GODS & DEMONS

Bell, book and candle are three major elements in the ritual of
exorcism. A fourth, salt, is held here by a grotesque figure.

A demon from the East: this fearsome figure
may represent Hayagriva, enemy of the gods
in both Buddhist and Hindu mythology and known
to Tibetan Buddhists as the 'Lord of Wrath'.

MYSTERIOUS FACTS
GODS & DEMONS

AMANDA O'NEILL

Grange BOOKS

CLB 3028

© 1993 Colour Library Books Ltd., Godalming, Surrey, England.

Published by Grange Books
An Imprint of Grange Books Limited
The Grange
Grange Yard
London
SE1 3AG

Published 1993

ISBN 1 85627 394 6

Printed and bound in Italy

The Author

Amanda O'Neill was born in Sussex, England, in 1951, and studied Anglo-Saxon, Old Norse, and Middle English literature at the University of Exeter. Her specialist field of interest lies in the Celtic myths and medieval romances of King Arthur. While working in educational administration at De Montfort University, Leicester, she has edited and written books on subjects ranging from the decorative arts to natural history. She was a contributor to *Lands and Peoples*, a multi-volume educational work published in Europe and the U.S.A. in 1990-1992. Her books on *Biblical Times* and *Ancient Times* have recently appeared in the U.S.A. and U.K., and she is engaged in a study of the history of domesticated animals and their association with humans.

Credits

Editor: Philip de Ste. Croix
Designer: Jill Coote
Picture research: Leora Kahn
Production: Ruth Arthur, Sally Connolly, Neil Randles
Director of Production: Gerald Hughes
Typesetting: SX Composing Ltd.
Colour separations: Scantrans Pte Ltd., Singapore
Printed and bound by New Interlitho SpA, Italy

Voodoo rites in Haiti: these worshippers have made a pilgrimage to offer up their prayers to Erzulie, goddess of love and bringer of good health and prosperity.

3/98
we

CONTENTS

Religious mysteries and miracles

To some readers it may seem strange, even wrong, that the first part of this book of 'Mysterious Facts' should deal with some of the beliefs of Christianity and other religions. Let us begin, therefore, by examining the original meaning of the word 'mystery'. It derives from the Greek words *mystos* ('keeping silence') and *myein* ('with closed eyes or lips'). In the ancient world – in Babylon, Egypt, Greece, Rome and elsewhere – the gods were worshipped through 'mysteries': groups of worshippers who formed 'secret societies' to preserve the purity of their beliefs. 'Mystery' came also to mean the truth of religious belief itself: the inner, central truth, which humans can never fully understand intellectually, but can know only through divine revelation. It is these 'mysteries' that the first part of this book examines.

Christianity is a late comer among the world's great religions, senior only to the Islamic faith. And just as Islam adopted some aspects of Christianity, such as belief in the Hebrew prophets and in Angels, so Christianity was influenced by the beliefs of the ancient world. It is not to belittle Judaeo-Christian beliefs that I have tried to show the connections between, for example, Persia's Ahura Mazda and Christianity's God the Father; between Mesopotamian and Babylonian heroes and the Biblical Noah. Rather it is to show that all religions that seek to raise up humanity tend towards similar 'mysteries'.

The peoples of the ancient world were closer than we are to nature, so it is not surprising that their gods often represented the most powerful natural forces they knew, from the Sun, Moon and other heavenly bodies to such strong or supposedly wise animals as the bull or serpent. I have tried to explain some of their beliefs, and although I describe some of the odder aspects

The folk of ancient Babylon feared Lilitu (who later appeared in the *Old Testament* as Lilith), a female demon who, as her attendant owls suggest, flew through the night sky to whip up storms and work evil.

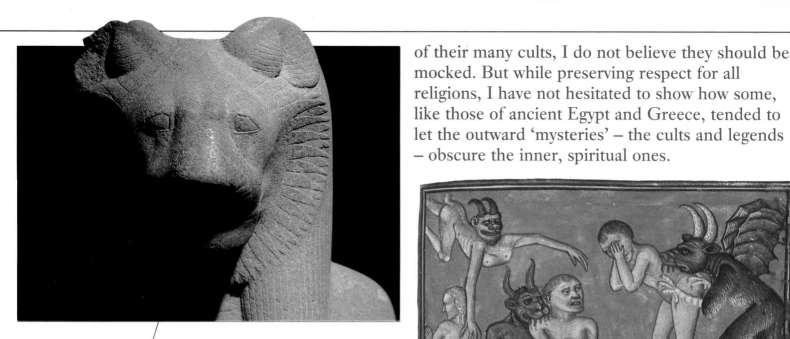

of their many cults, I do not believe they should be mocked. But while preserving respect for all religions, I have not hesitated to show how some, like those of ancient Egypt and Greece, tended to let the outward 'mysteries' – the cults and legends – obscure the inner, spiritual ones.

The ancient Egyptians identified lion-headed Sekhmet, wife of the god Ptah, with the merciless heat of the Sun, and made her a goddess of war and conquest.

Demons tear out the eyes of the damned: a 14th century artist's vision of Hell – a very real place for most Christians until very recent times.

Our Lady of Czestochowa, southern Poland, traditionally painted from life by St. Luke, is among the most famous of the world's many miracle working 'Black Madonnas'.

Miracle cures have occurred at the shrine of St. Cecilia at Trastevere, Rome – although she is now considered a legendary rather than real martyr of the early Church.

In reading of the beliefs our ancestors held on such subjects as Angels and demons, we must remember that their faith was simpler, and perhaps deeper, than ours. To them Heaven and Hell were real places, that could be described in detail and even mapped. We may think of them as superstitious – yet many people still believe in 'miracles', as my examination of modern Madonna cults and stigmatics shows. And what harm is there even in disputed miracles, like the famous Turin Shroud or 'Our Lady of Knock' (both of which sceptics dismiss as 'tourist attractions'), if they help to focus our attention on spiritual rather than material things?

Wise folk and witches

In contrast to the universal aspects of religious belief covered in the first part of this book, the second part begins with an examination of more localized beliefs and practices. They range from the old Druidic religion of the Celts of Western Europe to the mystical beliefs still held by some Aboriginal peoples in Australia; from the often bloody cults of the Vikings of Scandinavia and of Central and South American peoples before the European conquest to the animistic (based on nature) beliefs of traditional Japan and of Native American societies.

Western witches were said to use 'poppets' (French: *poupée*; 'doll'), like this 19th century British example, to call down curses on the persons in whose images they were made.

A shaman ('witch doctor') performs a ceremony. Such traditional healers and seers are found in many lands: this 'wise man' is at work in the Republic of Suriname, northeast South America.

Again, while not neglecting what are (to us) the stranger, and sometimes repellent, aspects of these beliefs, I have tried to show how much genuine religious feeling they embodied. Until quite recently it was common for 'educated', 'advanced' persons to dismiss the shamans ('wise' men and women; prophets and healers) of such peoples as the Inuit, Native Americans and, especially, the peoples of Black Africa, as 'medicine men' or 'witch doctors' – terms that carry with them the suggestion of primitive superstition or trickery. Today, we are becoming aware that the traditional wisdom, in particular herbal lore and techniques of meditation and 'mind expansion', preserved by such persons may be able to help cure some of the evils of our technological society.

A leading exponent of 'New Age' ideas, actress Shirley MacLaine (b.1934) is also well known for her writings on reincarnation and 'out of body experiences'.

Meditating in the Lotus posture, a girl seeks 'one-ness' with the universal spirit through the ancient Indian discipline of yoga (Sanskrit: *yog*; 'union').

to tabloid journalists than to the real power of Old Nick. But in the wrong hands, or in the wrong circumstances, the most innocent belief may be perverted. Germany's Nazis made use of occult beliefs and symbols in their climb to power; modern tyrants like Haiti's 'Papa Doc' Duvalier and some African dictators have held power by exploiting the religious beliefs of their peoples. Farther back in history, as I show in the final part of this section, Muslim and Hindu cults were transformed to mass murder movements, while in Europe and North America it was partly a reaction against 'free thinking', against harmless eccentrics who were judged to be a danger to society, that led to the execution of thousands of persons accused of witchcraft and the worship of Satan.

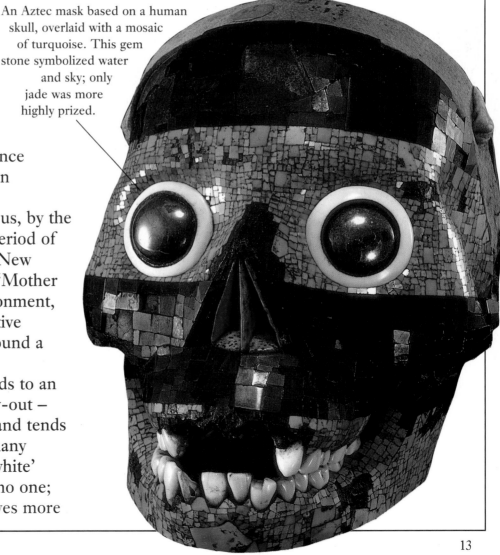

An Aztec mask based on a human skull, overlaid with a mosaic of turquoise. This gem stone symbolized water and sky; only jade was more highly prized.

Some of this re-evaluation of wisdom once ignored by the sophisticated West has been triggered by the growth of the 'New Age' movement, ushered in, its enthusiasts tell us, by the dawning of the 'age of Aquarius', a new period of spiritual growth. I see much to admire in New Agers' advocacy of respect for the Earth ('Mother Gaia'), in their true concern for the environment, and in their willingness to explore alternative medical techniques. But I would like to sound a warning note.

Taken to the extreme, New Ageism leads to an exaggerated respect for the weird and way-out – simply because it is weird and way-out – and tends towards 'cultism'. There are, of course, many harmless modern cults: Wicca (modern 'white' witchcraft) has, so far as I know, harmed no one; the 'evil' of modern Satanism probably owes more

Fairies, sprites and spooks

'All argument is against it; but all belief is for it'. That was the view of the supernatural taken by the great 18th century thinker Dr. Samuel Johnson (whose investigation of a ghost with the splendid name of 'Scratching Fanny' features with other ghostly tales in the last part of this book). He was, I think, right in thinking that most of us wish to believe in the supernatural – but since Johnson's time the work of psychic researchers has provided many more arguments in favour of such belief.

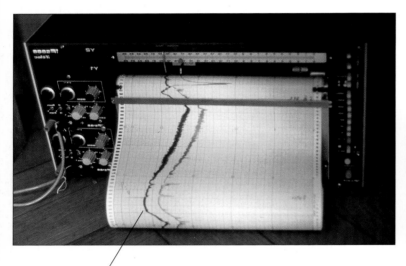

Hunting ghosts with modern technology: inexplicable changes in temperature were recorded when this machine was used to monitor an apartment plagued by poltergeists at Mulhouse, France.

With the mass of evidence gathered, it is hard to deny the existence of poltergeists: unseen but noisy spirits, perhaps created by 'pyschic energy' released by troubled teenagers or disturbed persons, whose pranks sometimes take a sinister turn. The traditional ghost of Gothick fiction – the white sheeted, moaning, chain rattling spook – has become a comic cliché, but too many rational, impartial persons have reported 'ghostly' experiences for us to dismiss all such accounts as products of overripe imagination or overheated emotion.

Ghosts may be divided into two major categories: 'hauntings' and 'apparitions'. Hauntings are appearances of persons known to be dead. They may be repeated many times over a period of years, even centuries, but tend gradually to 'fade' with time. Some believe they are caused by 'mental imprints' of violent events and great emotions; that such things are somehow 'recorded' and may 'play back' from time to time. Certainly, among the most commonly reported hauntings are the appearances of suicides, murder victims, soldiers killed in battle and the like.

More common, and perhaps more easily credited, are 'apparitions': single supernatural appearances of persons who may be either dead or

A modern ghost? This strange, 'shrouded' image appeared when a time exposure photograph of Limassol Bay, Cyprus, was developed in 1986.

Typical example of a 'spirit' photograph of the Victorian period, c.1890. Perhaps it is genuine – but it is obvious that it could easily be faked.

still alive. Typically, the figure of a person at the point of death appears to tell a close relative or friend of the event, or to deliver a warning or message. Apparitions of the living, sometimes interpreted as unconscious telepathic messages that take on physical shape to the mind of the receiver, usually appear to loved ones at times of crisis.

A photograph taken in 1878, at a Spiritualist séance where a medium called Eglington claimed to have materialized this figure in Arabic dress.

A headless 'ghost dog', unseen by the photographer at the time, appeared in a picture taken by a retired British police inspector, c.1916.

Joe Groombridge (father of Richard O'Neill, the author of two other books in this series) had a typical experience of an apparition of a living person. Early in World War II he was a tank driver with an armoured unit in the North African desert campaign. In a skirmish near Tobruk his tank was hit and he was wounded and knocked unconscious. He came round to hear a voice calling: 'Wake up, Dadda; you must wake up!' Through the driver's eye slot he saw the figure of his 4-year-old son Richard urging: 'Get out, Dadda; get out quickly!' Joe dragged himself from the tank – a few seconds before it was hit again and 'brewed up' into a flaming wreck. As Joe said, it was probably his subconscious that told him a stationary tank under heavy shellfire was no place to be; but he was certain that he had seen and heard Richard – who has absolutely no memory of the event.

God the Father: God the Mother

Humankind created gods in its own image. Perhaps the oldest portrayals are Stone Age 'Venuses', stylized statuettes of pregnant women with huge breasts, bellies and thighs: the Mother Goddess at her most basic. From this crude image of maternity sprang the queenly goddesses of the ancient world: Phoenician Astarte, Phrygian Cybele, Babylonian Ishtar, Thracian Bendis, Cretan Rhea and Egyptian Isis. Deities not just of fertility but of sexual love, most are models of female beauty, like Aphrodite of Greece. But the Goddess may also be super-feminine (many-breasted Diana of the Ephesians); part masculine (bearded Ishtar of Assyria, 'lady of battles'); or even multiple (the Celtic trinity of Mothers). In many later cultures the Mother was forced to yield place as 'Supreme Being' to a male Creator. But often the divine Father remained a background figure, while people gave more active worship to gods of fertility or war. Thus Mesopotamia's central deity was Baal ('Lord'), the young, virile rain god, not the aged, all-knowing 'supreme god' El, while the Celts' 'all-father', the Dagda ('Good God'), was a shadowy, even comic figure – a fat, greedy man. In Europe the sky god Dyaus Pitar ('Divine One') replaced the Mother as Creator from about 2000 B.C. As Greek Zeus or Roman Jupiter he displays very human characteristics: ancient myths tell how the 'father of men' often visited mortals – usually to seduce their women. In Northern Europe, the 'All-father' was the wind god Odin. Like Zeus, Odin travelled among men; but this sinister, one-eyed figure, in great grey cloak and slouch hat, was an inconstant lord who often betrayed his followers. More enduring than any were the faceless gods of two religions that forbade the portrayal of Godhead: the Jews' Jehovah and the Muslims' Allah.

In the Classical world the love goddess (Greek Aphrodite or Roman Venus) was an ideal of female beauty far removed from maternity – and a wanton, jealous and vengeful deity who brought strife among gods and mortals alike.

The Israelite leader Moses saw God, not as a physical presence but represented by a burning bush. His people were among the first to conceive of a God without bodily form.

Christianity never quite destroyed the cult of the Celtic Mother Goddess. Across Britain, country churches feature her ugly yet powerful images, unrepentantly pagan and sometimes rampantly sexual.

This early bronze bust of a Canaanite fertility god (probably Baal) depicts Godhead via a simple phallic shape rather than as an image of human beauty.

Farmers in Canaan relied on rain god Baal to fend off Mot, deity of death and sterility.

❑ Christmas Eve was once the Celtic festival of *Modraniht*, 'night of the Mothers'. The cult of the Mothers died hard. In the 11th century Bishop Burchard of Worms, Germany, had to rebuke women of his church for their stubborn belief in three divine women called the *Parcae* – for whom they ritually laid three places at table.

❑ Norse god Odin (above) is credited with the highly practical wisdom of *Hávámal* (a kind of Norse *Book of Proverbs*), which counsels warriors not to sit with their backs to a door, and not to waste a whole loaf on a friend who will happily accept half.

❑ The Babylonian cult of Ishtar required every woman once in her life to lie with a stranger at the temple as an act of worship, reflecting the goddess's dual nature as Mother and 'prostitute compassionate'. Greek historian Herodotus (c.484-425 B.C.), who was shocked by the custom, tells us that pretty women quickly fulfilled their duty, but 'the uncomely sometimes have to wait several years'.

The life everlasting

'Don't mourn for me now, don't mourn for me never: I'm going to do nothing for ever and ever'. The hardworked housewife's epitaph depicts Heaven simply as a place of rest. Many religions have held much the same view, seeing Heaven as a land of ease in reward for virtue and as compensation for life's hardships. For Ancient Egyptians it was a farmers' paradise, a fertile Land of the Blessed where nature's abundance meant no need to labour; Native American peoples looked to the Happy Hunting Grounds, a hunters' Heaven. The Islamic peoples of the arid Middle East saw Paradise as a perfect oasis garden, with rivers of pure water, milk, wine and honey, where blessed souls relaxed in silken robes, served by beautiful maidens. Warlike Vikings aspired to Valhalla, Hall of the Slain: the ultimate banquet hall, with warm fires, unlimited pork and mead, and daily battles – from which the dead rose each night to join their slayers at the feast. Some religions took a more spiritual view. Buddhism and Hinduism see Heaven not as an end in itself but as part of the cycle of rebirth through which the soul passes. Indian Buddhists believe souls progress through 26 Heavens. The lower ones offer sensual rewards: golden palaces equipped with every luxury from divine food to dancing girls. From these pleasures, souls graduate to higher Heavens of worship and meditation. The Heaven of Christianity is meant to be another spiritual one, of everlasting bliss in God's kingdom; but at various times it has been described in terms of more earthly rewards. Although Christians have never been offered concubines or alcohol in heaven, one of the delights they were promised by the medieval church was that of gloating, in most un-Christian spirit, over the pains of sinners in Hell below.

The Christian Paradise: an enchanted garden where men and women – and animals – return to the primeval innocence of Eden.

The Eight Immortals of China: sages who, Confucianists and Taoists hold, won the goal of the virtuous – not Heaven, but unity with Heaven and Earth as a perfected Immortal.

Far from the bustle of earthly life, perfected souls are freed from the curse of labour laid on Adam and Eve and their descendants.

Heaven rewards the just. Here the Prophet Muhammad ascends to a warm welcome in Paradise, greeted by Angels laden with gifts, fine raiment and banquet dishes.

Viking heroes expected to pay for afterlife hospitality in Valhalla by backing the gods in a cosmic battle at the end of the world.

They faced no ordinary foes, but the monstrous wolf Fenrisulfr, his brother the World Serpent, and a rampaging mob of fire giants.

FACT FILE

❑ As late as the 6th century A.D., many Europeans believed the souls of the dead voyaged to Britain, summoning the men of Brittany, France, to ferry them over the English Channel. Breton fishermen said their boats at night were laden with invisible passengers whose weight made the boats ride low in the water.

❑ The Aztec Heaven – the 'Mansion of the Sun' – was reserved for priests and nobles. Their lower classes could expect no such comfort in the afterlife; which may explain why Aztec peasants welcomed Christian priests, who said Heaven was won by baptism, not social status.

❑ The rewards of the Muslim paradise include lovely virgins as wives. Legend says Muhammad promised his friend Zayd paradise for marrying an old woman. When the prophet visited paradise, he met a fair maiden who told him she belonged to Zayd.

❑ In 1246 a shocked Franciscan monk found that Genghis Khan's Mongol warriors 'know nothing of everlasting life and eternal damnation, but they believe that after death they will live in another world and increase their flocks, and eat and drink and do the other things which are done by men in this world'. So Mongol dead were outfitted as for an earthly journey, with tents, food, clothing, money, servants and concubines.

Angelic hosts of Heaven

Angels and, as seen here, the spirits of old English archers, were said to have appeared to support British soldiers at Mons in 1914.

Gods like Zeus and Odin had human characteristics, and often took earthly forms to interact directly with mortals. Not so the unseen deities of Judaism and Islam, Jehovah and Allah, who spoke to men through divine spirits called Angels (from the Greek word for 'messenger'). *The Bible* tells how God sent Angels to halt Abraham's sacrifice of Isaac, and to announce the coming of Jesus to Mary. Angels also form the Heavenly court, worshipping at God's throne. As pure spirits, they lack bodies, although convention depicts them in beautiful human form, with wings and white robes. The medieval Christian Church evolved an elaborate 'Angelology': its scholars, addicted to classifying and counting, worked out a pecking order of ranks and functions. Most agreed on nine angelic orders: Seraphim, Cherubim, Thrones, Dominions, Virtues, Powers, Principalities, Archangels and Angels. Highest ranking were Angels of the Presence, God's attendants: lower ranks tended human affairs.

A blast on a trumpet by an Angel (Gabriel say Christians, but Muslims favour Israfel) will herald the Day of Judgement.

Theologians described a civil war in Heaven, when the Angel Lucifer led a rebellion against God – and was cast out, to become Satan. We are told that Angels visited early Christian saints, and the Prophet of Islam, Muhammad. But today Angel visits are rare. The last major angelic intervention in human affairs was reported in 1914 in the London *Evening News*, which told (with eyewitness reports) how Angels appeared to hearten British troops in the desperate rearguard action at Mons, early in World War I. Years later, author Arthur Machen revealed it had been a propaganda exercise based on his short story telling how the spirits of bowmen from Agincourt (Britain's great victory in France in 1415) had come to fight alongside their descendants. But even soldiers who had themselves fought at Mons credited the story, and later swore they had seen Angels.

Our idea of Angels as graceful, winged beings largely stems from paintings by masters like Simone Martini, who portrayed the Archangel Gabriel in this *Annunciation* of c.1333.

The Archangel Michael appears in *The Bible's* *Old* and *New* *Testaments*.

Michael, traditionally the 'captain of the heavenly host', is seen weighing out human souls on Judgement Day in a 15th century painting.

Angels in an old Persian manuscript: the Muslim faith shares with Christianity a belief in Angels, who visited the Prophet Muhammad.

The Blessed Virgin is at first alarmed by the angelic messenger's news that she is to bear the Son of God.

The legions of the damned

The Devil we know – horned, hoofed, smelling of sulphur and 'black as Satan' – was designed by Pope Gregory the Great (c.540-604). But his roots are much older, going back to Ahriman ('Destructive Thought'), Persian god of evil and forebear of Judaism's Satan. Unlike Ahriman, Satan was no equal rival to God, but an adversary temporarily tolerated as part of the divine plan. Christianity inherited and developed this idea, giving the Evil One attributes from a range of pagan gods. Pope Gregory borrowed the horns and hoofs of the Greek god Pan, Roman Vulcan's lameness and Saturn's blackness, and Norse Thor's beard and sulphuric smell. Other gods, mostly those of Old Testament times, such as Beelzebub, Asmodeus and Astaroth, provided the names for Satan's demon followers. Satan himself was identified with rebel Angel Lucifer, who led a war in Heaven and was cast out to Hell with his followers. By the 14th century he was seen as 'Arch-enemy' of God and man, aided and abetted by demons 'as numerous as bees' (their number variously reckoned by medieval churchmen as between 7,405,926 and 133,306,668) ranked in a hierarchy which aped the Church's. His portrait was expanded with lurid details of his anatomy and habits (notably sexual), meant to frighten people into virtue. This could work the wrong way: the powerful image drew some to devil-worship and witchcraft. Many tales tell how magicians strove to control demons, or signed pacts with the Devil, trading their souls for worldly wealth. Satanic cults still exist, though only a minority takes them seriously. To the Church, Satan's role, tempting mortals to sin and overseeing the torments of Hell, is simply part of God's plan: 'The demons are our Lord's bailiffs, whom he hath set apart to exercise men', explained St. Francis of Assisi (1181-1226).

Many magicians have tried to call up demons to aid them. 'Lucifuge Rofocale', as this medieval style illustration suggests, was invoked by those who hoped to find buried treasure.

Horrific demons and monsters people Hell in the fearsome vision of Pieter Breughel the Elder (c.1525-69).

A 12th century carving at the Church of San Zeno, Verona, Italy, shows Saint Zeno (d.c.372) exorcizing a woman possessed by a demon – which is leaving by way of her mouth.

An Angel in medieval armour, presumably Archangel Michael, traditionally the leader of the heavenly host, heads the battle against the demons.

The painter meant these grotesque figures to represent the fallen Angels, cast into Hell for their revolt against God.

It is in this form, as the 'Sabbatic Goat', that the Devil is said to have joined witches at their meetings (Sabbats). The picture is based on a drawing by the famous French occultist Eliphas Lévi (1810-75).

FACT FILE

❑ The Greeks believed demons were mortal, but much longer lived than humans. Plutarch (c.A.D.46-120) said a demon lived 9,720 years – but was liable, like humans, to become old and infirm. Some 800 years earlier, the poet Hesiod credited demons with a lifespan 10 times that of the Phoenix, which lived 972 times as long as man: demonic life expectancy was therefore 680,000 years.

❑ Specialist fiends included incubi and succubi, demon lovers which took human form – often that of the victim's spouse or lover. Many a pregnant nun and unfaithful wife in the Middle Ages saved her name by claiming rape by an incubus. Legend says Merlin the magician owed his supernatural powers to being sired by an incubus.

❑ In Central America in the 18th century the Church condemned chocolate as a snare of the Devil – and punished those caught drinking chocolate by excommunication.

❑ The *New Testament* tells how Satan tried to tempt Jesus with the rewards of an earthly kingdom. Similarly, Buddhist tradition says the demon Mara tried to stop Buddha bringing enlightenment to humankind. The human race, said Mara, was not ready for Buddha's teachings: he might as well pass on to Nirvana (the Buddhist Heaven).

The terrors of Hell

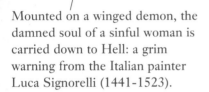

Many ancient religions never troubled to design elaborate afterworlds, but taught of an existence after death which can only be described as deathly dull. Their lands of the dead – like the ancient Greeks' Hades, or the old Hebrews' Sheol – were sad, dull, shadowy places where souls wandered aimlessly and endlessly. Later, more sophisticated creeds developed the idea of a place of punishment for souls. Late Judaism introduced Gehenna, a place of 'gloomy fire always burning', named after the spot where Jerusalem's garbage was burned. Hinduism and some forms of Buddhism go much farther. Hindu scriptures tell of 100,000 Hells, each purpose-made to punish a particular crime with horrid torments: souls are ground between millstones, cast on to knives and so on. Buddhism also has many Hells equipped with fearful tortures: it is said that merely to describe them would take 100,000 years. But both Hinduism and Buddhism see existence as a never-ending cycle of rebirth; so punishment after death is severe, but not unending. When the soul has served its sentence it is freed, to be reborn in a lower life form. Islam too promises sinners torment in Hell – but with an escape clause: Allah the All-Merciful pardons the sincerely repentant even in the midst of Hell. It was Christianity that took the horrors of Hell to their ultimate by making them eternal. The true Christian Hell is the spiritual agony of exile from God; but during the Middle Ages it was elaborated in ever more sadistic and grotesquely realistic terms. Then the Church aimed to terrorize people into virtue, and much of the artistic and literary ingenuity of the Middle Ages was devoted to picturing the cruellest afterworld of any world religion.

Mounted on a winged demon, the damned soul of a sinful woman is carried down to Hell: a grim warning from the Italian painter Luca Signorelli (1441-1523).

The damned souls are condemned to eternal torment. 'Hellfire' was a real terror for most medieval folk, and artist Hans Memling (c.1430-94) was probably no exception.

Bérenger Saunière (d.1917), the priest who designed this demon figure for his church at Rennes-le-Château, France, was said to have found a great treasure – perhaps with unholy aid – and to have died a millionaire.

Merciless demons, one in the form of a grinning ape, inflict the punishment decreed by God. Such horrific pictures were intended to terrify people into good Christian behaviour.

This bestial demon is from the *Infernal Dictionary* of French 'demonologist' Collin de Plancy (1793-1887), an expert in the field.

Taloned hands and feet, tail and leopard's head characterize the minor demon 'Flauros'.

❑ The ancient Greek underworld (below), realm of Hades, was a desolate land ringed by five rivers, including the (mythical) Styx and (real) Acheron. The dead were buried with a coin to pay the ferry over the waters – or must wander the banks of Acheron forever. By classical times, Hades incorporated judgement after death: the good were rewarded by bliss in the Elysian Fields; the sinners punished in Tartarus.

❑ Norse warriors believed souls not chosen to enter Valhalla went to a desolate land ruled by the goddess Hel. The destination of a man's soul did not depend on whether he had lived a virtuous life, but on how he died. Death by violence – in battle or as a sacrifice – was the way to Valhalla. Death from sickness or old age led the soul to Hel's bleak realm.

❑ Medieval clerics studied Hell's geography. A German divine stated 100 billion souls, packed tightly 'like anchovies', would fit into a cubic mile. Perhaps the Jesuit Cornelius à Lapide used similar figures to work out that Hell was only 200 Italian miles across.

Holy Mother and Holy Son

The holy love of the Mother for her Child is so miraculously portrayed by artists like Botticelli that it is no wonder millions have sought the Blessed Virgin's aid.

Although Church authorities are often loath to endorse them, and sceptics speak of mass hallucinations, there are many well attested reports of apparitions of the Virgin Mary, and of miraculous images of her. 'Weeping', 'bleeding' or 'moving' Madonnas are reported worldwide, ranging from icons in ancient European churches to plaster statuettes in U.S. mobile homes. Her most famous appearances have been in 1858 at Lourdes, France, where she revealed healing waters to St. Bernadette, and at Fátima, Portugal, in 1917. There, although only three peasant girls saw her, c.70,000 persons witnessed a meteorological phenomenon ('dance of the Sun') she had promised. It is said the Virgin of Fátima made a revelation, for the Pope's ears only, foretelling global catastrophe, and that in 1960 Pope John XXIII told Vatican officials it made him 'weak with horror'. Manifestations of the Virgin's Holy Son include the stigmata (Greek: 'brands'), wounds like those of the crucified Christ, that appear on some holy persons. Padre Pio (1887-1968), a monk of Foggia, Italy, bled from hands, feet and side from 1918 until his death – when the wounds vanished. Sister Elena Aiello (d.1961), another Italian monastic, bled from her hands. Blood spots on the wall of her room formed a face of Christ which itself exuded blood that tests showed to be human. It has been suggested that stigmata are caused by autosuggestion, from within the stigmatic's own mind: in the case of monastics, from their long contemplation of Christ's agonies. Sceptics say that just as most apparitions of the Virgin are to young girls, who describe her conventionally as a young, beautiful woman in blue robes, so stigmata appear on the palms and soles – where Christ is traditionally shown as being nailed – rather than on wrists and ankles, where the nails would have been driven in a Roman crucifixion.

The hands of Antonio Ruffini (seen here in 1987) have borne stigmata since he was granted a vision of the Virgin near Rome in 1951.

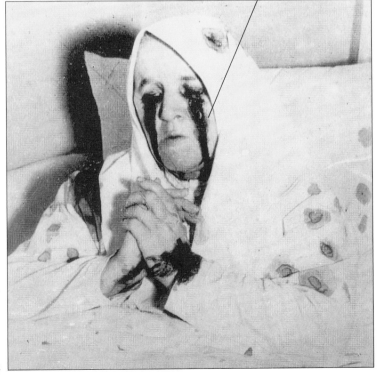

In 1879 the Virgin appeared at the Roman Catholic church at Knock, Co. Mayo, Ireland. Later, after reports of miraculous cures, Knock became a pilgrimage centre: a new church to hold 7,500 worshippers was built in 1974; the Pope visited in 1979; and in 1986 an international airport was opened at nearby Charlestown to handle some 1,000,000 pilgims each year.

Believers worldwide say that many images of the Virgin, like this one in Brooklyn, N.Y., 1984, have wept for sinful, suffering humanity.

A Brazilian 'Black Madonna'. In Europe, some dark skinned images of the Virgin are said to be miracle working..

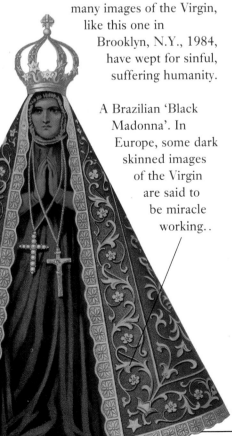

Teresa Neumann of Bavaria, Germany, received the stigmata after a vision in 1926. Every Friday until her death in 1962 she bled from hands, side, feet and forehead.

Worried by huge crowds flocking to Padre Pio (above) and by large sums sent him by admirers (he was released from his monk's vow of poverty, but gave all donations to charity) the Roman Church twice suspended Padre Pio from religious duties. As well as a stigmatic, he was a clairvoyant and healer: tests showed that in trance state his body temperature rose to 48°C.(118.4°F.). Calls for his canonization are opposed by some Church authorities.

Gods of ancient empires

Pazuzu, a demon feared by the Assyrians, who dominated the area of Mesopotamia in c.1300-600 B.C. They worshipped the goddess Ishtar.

Like the demons of traditional Christian belief, Pazuzu is shown with claws, wings and horns.

Historians call Mesopotamia's Tigris-Euphrates valley the 'cradle of civilization'. It saw the first farmers in c.8000 B.C., the earliest towns, and, by c.3500 B.C., the sophisticated Sumerian Empire. The development of writing in Sumer allows us knowledge of some of humanity's first gods, handed down by Sumer to the successive empires of Akkadia (after c.2300 B.C.) and Babylon (from c.1990 B.C.). The deities are those of a farming culture dependent on rivers, and honour the powers of nature. At the centre of the ancient empires' pantheon were neither Mother Goddess nor Sky-Father – but gods who, tiring of tilling the soil and digging canals, created mortals to do it for them. A huge family of gods was ruled by three great ones: heaven-god An; air-god Enlil; and mother-goddess Ninhursag. Enlil ruled the land where folk labour: his chief gift to humanity was the pickaxe, the tool that built canals and cities. Babylon kept Sumer's basiç theology, but made a local god Marduk ('bull calf of the sun') its chief deity. Sumer's Creation Myth was expanded into Babylon's epic *Poem of Creation* (known from its opening as *Enuma elish*; 'When on high') in which Marduk became the Creator who slew the ocean-dragon to form Heaven and Earth from her body. Its importance is apparent from the large number of copies surviving, dating from c.900-200 B.C. Mesopotamian myths have intriguing parallels with the *Old Testament*. The tale of water god Enki, cursed by the mother goddess for eating forbidden plants in Dilmun (Paradise), recalls to us Adam's fall in Eden. Another myth tells how the gods punished humanity with a worldwide Flood, and how the virtuous Ziusudra, warned by Enki, built a boat and, like Noah, preserved his family.

Marduk, champion of the gods, is seen in combat with Tiamat, whom he slew, in an illustration based on an ancient Assyrian carving showing the story of the Creation.

Symbols of sun god Shamash, moon god Sin, and another Mesopotamian deity are at the head of a Babylonian stele (memorial tablet) of around the 9th century B.C.

Tiamat, the fearsome, female dragon of Babylonian myth, lived in the salt water of the ocean. The people of Mesopotamia recognized this as the original source of all life.

Babylonian script: the art of writing was first developed in Mesopotamia c.5,000 years ago.

Fish-tailed Dagon was the sea god of the Philistines from c.1200 B.C. He is sometimes quite wrongly identified with the Mesopotamian fertility god, Dagan.

29

Gilgamesh, the first super-hero

In 1857 scholars cracked the code of Babylonian cuneiform ('wedge shaped writing', from its symbols) and began to read texts from ancient Mesopotamia. Soon they deciphered clay tablets of the 7th century B.C. from the Assyrian royal library of Nineveh, and rediscovered the world's first 'best seller', the *Epic of Gilgamesh*. Gilgamesh was king of the Sumerian city of Uruk, c.2700 B.C. Tradition says he rebuilt Uruk – probably true, since he reigned in Sumer's great age of temple-building – and the survival of his name alone tells us he was a ruler whose works and personality were out of the ordinary. There history ends and myth begins. The mythic Gilgamesh is no mortal king but 'most glorious of the heroes'; the epic, far from factual biography, explores the ageless theme of man's dread of death. Gilgamesh is a super-hero, son of a goddess and a mortal man. At the outset he has yet to control his semi-divine nature: he is a tearaway who slays young men and ravishes women. He is transformed when the gods create a fit companion for him: Enkidu, the 'wild man', who must be tamed to become the hero's inseparable friend. Together they perform great feats, destroying the giant Humbaba and the monstrous Bull of Heaven. Then death claims Enkidu. Gilgamesh, alone again, realizes, 'What my brother is now, that shall I be when I am dead', and sets out on a quest for immortality. Almost he succeeds: at last, and inevitably, he fails. Returning to Uruk, he recognizes that death is all men's destiny: the only immortality is fame, by which a man's name lives on. The story of Gilgamesh's heroic yet doomed quest spoke directly to the embattled pessimism of Mesopotamia's peoples. It was retold through successive empires, over more than seven centuries: versions survive in Sumerian, Old Babylonian, Hittite, Hurrian, Akkadian and Assyrian.

Sumerian superman Gilgamesh, hero of the world's first great epic, carries a lion in an 8th century B.C. carving from the palace of Sargon II, at Khorsabad, modern Iraq.

Gilgamesh was ruler of Uruk (modern Erech, Iraq) in c.2700 B.C. This gold dagger from nearby Ur dates from around the same period.

A gold bull's head with beard of lapis lazuli, found at Ur, is mounted on a reconstructed stringed instrument of the time.

An intricately made scabbard provides a fitting sheath for so precious a weapon.

Court musicians at Uruk and other Sumerian cities used instruments like this lyre (harp), carved with gods and heroes, to sing the praises of Gilgamesh and other rulers.

Goddess Ishtar (Astarte), seen here on an 8th century B.C. relief, was angry when Gilgamesh refused her offer of love and set the monstrous Bull of Heaven on him.

FACT FILE

❏ Biblical scholars were astounded to find in the *Epic of Gilgamesh* a Flood myth comparable to that in *Genesis*. Utnapishtim, parallel to Biblical Noah, tells Gilgamesh how the gods punished mankind with a Flood, and how he was warned by the god Enki to build an 'Ark' (below) to save himself and his family. The story's details match those of *Genesis*: historians believe both reflect ancient tribal memory. But the conclusion differs: the One God's covenant with his servant Noah is replaced by dispute among the gods.

❏ Some scholars see the story of Enkidu as an allegory of human progress from savagery to civilization. He begins as a wild man, living with beasts. When frightened locals engage a city harlot to seduce him, the animals reject him. Gradually he enters the world of men, first as a shepherd, finally entering the city of Uruk to become a hero. But on his deathbed he looks back to his old, wild life and curses those who educated him.

Egypt's cult of the dead

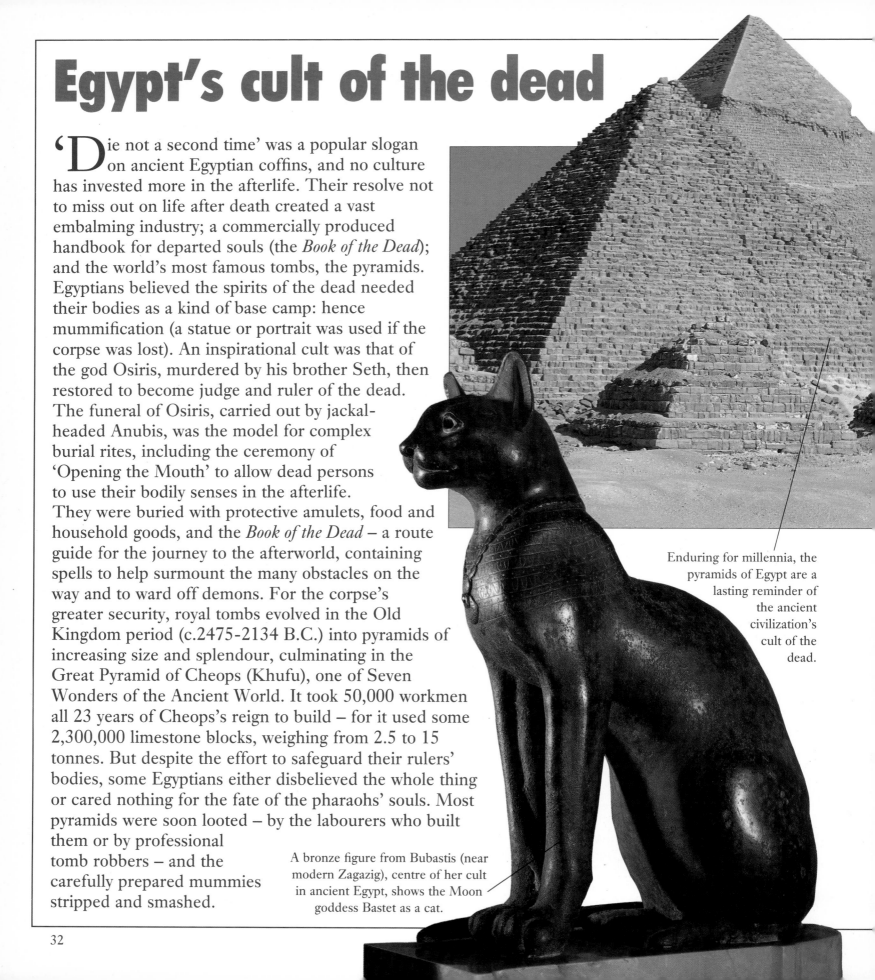

'Die not a second time' was a popular slogan on ancient Egyptian coffins, and no culture has invested more in the afterlife. Their resolve not to miss out on life after death created a vast embalming industry; a commercially produced handbook for departed souls (the *Book of the Dead*); and the world's most famous tombs, the pyramids. Egyptians believed the spirits of the dead needed their bodies as a kind of base camp: hence mummification (a statue or portrait was used if the corpse was lost). An inspirational cult was that of the god Osiris, murdered by his brother Seth, then restored to become judge and ruler of the dead. The funeral of Osiris, carried out by jackal-headed Anubis, was the model for complex burial rites, including the ceremony of 'Opening the Mouth' to allow dead persons to use their bodily senses in the afterlife. They were buried with protective amulets, food and household goods, and the *Book of the Dead* – a route guide for the journey to the afterworld, containing spells to help surmount the many obstacles on the way and to ward off demons. For the corpse's greater security, royal tombs evolved in the Old Kingdom period (c.2475-2134 B.C.) into pyramids of increasing size and splendour, culminating in the Great Pyramid of Cheops (Khufu), one of Seven Wonders of the Ancient World. It took 50,000 workmen all 23 years of Cheops's reign to build – for it used some 2,300,000 limestone blocks, weighing from 2.5 to 15 tonnes. But despite the effort to safeguard their rulers' bodies, some Egyptians either disbelieved the whole thing or cared nothing for the fate of the pharaohs' souls. Most pyramids were soon looted – by the labourers who built them or by professional tomb robbers – and the carefully prepared mummies stripped and smashed.

Enduring for millennia, the pyramids of Egypt are a lasting reminder of the ancient civilization's cult of the dead.

A bronze figure from Bubastis (near modern Zagazig), centre of her cult in ancient Egypt, shows the Moon goddess Bastet as a cat.

The Book of the Dead, laying down what must done to ensure life after death, was buried with every notable person.

Ram-headed Sphinxes line an avenue in the great temple complex at Luxor (Al Uqsor; ancient Thebes). Sphinxes ('Stranglers') were guardian figures in ancient Egypt.

Anubis, jackal-headed god of funerals, supports a pharaoh's mummy case as his wife, daughter and servants look on in adoration.

❏ Mystics have theorized that the dimensions of the Great Pyramid foretell the future. One pyramidologist 'read' its Grand Gallery as a record of the history of Christianity, with emphasis on the British Church – since, he said, it was built by a 'lost tribe of Israel', ancestors of the British race. Others claim pyramids have preservative powers, keeping bodies undecayed and food fresh. Scientists deny 'pyramid power', but believers sit in model pyramids (above) to cure toothache or calm the mind. In 1991 the British press reported that members of the Royal family had tried this New Age therapy.

❏ Expert mummification was a 70-day job: removing organs for separate burial in jars, drying the corpse with natron (a kind of rock salt), and cosmetic treatment that included mud packs under the skin to plump it out. Then the mummy was wrapped in up to 2.5km (1.5mi) of linen bandages. Later embalmers grew slipshod. Fine packaging often hid a body so ill-preserved it had fallen to bits and been reassembled – using bits of other corpses.

Soap opera on Mount Olympus

The gods of ancient Greece and Rome were immortals with very human personalities – so human that classical myths read like divine soap opera. On Mount Olympus, the king of the gods, Greek Zeus or Roman Jupiter, headed a bickering family addicted to intrigue and adultery. Their interference in mortals' affairs was arbitrary: aiding favourites; persecuting those who offended them. The Greeks hit a fine balance between their 'humanized' gods and religious belief. They enjoyed stories of sex and power, like that of blacksmith god Hephaistos catching his wife Aphrodite, goddess of love, in bed with her lover Ares, god of war. But they solemnly worshipped the same gods at temples, local shrines and oracles. At last soap opera and faith proved incompatible. When Greek philosophers began to set reason against myth, even the death sentence passed on Socrates for impiety could not wipe out the influence of that 'midwife of men's thoughts'. In Rome the state religion became a political tool. It boosted Roman superiority over subject peoples by making the emperors gods – usually after their deaths, although the insane Caligula deified himself. But for those who sought something deeper, there were mystery cults, reserved for initiates. In Greece these included the secret rites of corn goddess Demeter, and the orgiastic feasts of wine god Dionysos, whose female followers, Maenads ('wild women'), were said to tear wild beasts and even men to pieces. These uninhibited rites shocked Rome into banning the Dionysian cult in 186 B.C., and executing thousands of worshippers. But Rome had its own mystery religion, Mithraism, a cult of soldiers, for whom it was a 'secret society' much like modern Freemasonry. Others in Rome turned to a new religion that also offered personal salvation: Christianity.

A statue of c.100 B.C. shows Aphrodite (Roman: Venus), goddess of love, as the period's ideal woman.

God of sexual love: Eros (Roman: Cupid), Aphrodite's son. Seen as a winged child, he is often shown with a bow and 'arrows of desire'.

A goat's legs and horns mark lustful Pan, god of pastures and herds. Angered, he struck humans with sudden fear: 'panic'.

Poseidon (Roman: Neptune) was the god of the seas, armed with a magical trident made by the Cyclopes, a race of one-eyed giants.

'Sky father' Zeus (Roman: Jupiter), king of the gods and master of the weather, is portrayed as a handsome, mature man in this noble sculpture dating from the 5th century B.C.

A mosaic from the Roman city of Pompeii, destroyed by an earthquake in A.D. 79, portrays Demeter (Roman: Ceres), the goddess of Earth's fruitfulness.

❏ Animal sacrifices to the gods were made regularly, with special offerings in thanks for special favours. This caused the Athenians some embarrassment after their victory at the battle of Marathon (490 B.C.). Before the battle, they promised the goddess Artemis as many goats as they slew Persians. The slaughter was so colossal that they did not have enough goats, and had to pay off the goddess at the rate of 500 goats each year.

❏ The cult of the god Mithra (above), who brought fertility to the world by slaying a divine bull, came from Persia – brought to Rome, says historian Plutarch, in 67 B.C. by captured pirates. Lord of battles, Mithra had a special appeal to Roman soldiers, who spread his cult across the Empire. Mithraism had much in common with Christianity in both ethics and rituals – and seemed to Christians a Satanic travesty of their faith. Christianity won, but a Mithraic echo lingers in the date of Christmas Day: December 25 was the feast of Mithra's birth.

The bull as god and monster

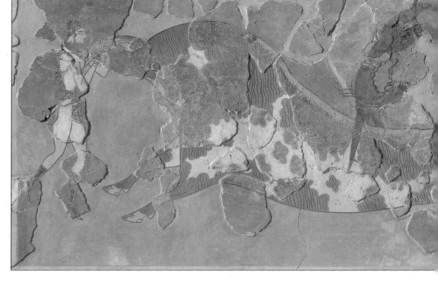

Our ancestors saw gods at work in the forces of nature. In many parts of the world they developed a cult of the bull: a beast whose strength and sexual potency impressed hunters and farmers alike. Its image figures much in Stone Age cave paintings in Europe and was immortalized on the walls of Babylon in 600 B.C. Slain by the god Mithra, it became the symbol of the Mithraic faith – equivalent to Christianity's Cross. In Egypt the bull was supreme among sacred animals – particularly the Apis bull, which was held to be the god Ptah incarnate and was housed royally in a temple at Memphis, with human servants and a harem of concubine cows: when it died, its successor was recognized by its markings. Another bull cult inspired the Greek myth of the hero Theseus and the Minotaur: a bull-headed monster, unnatural offspring of Pasiphae, wife of King Minos of Crete, by a bull. Minos kept this brute in an impenetrable maze, the Labyrinth, and demanded annual tribute of 14 young Athenians to feed it. Theseus, son of King Aegeus of Athens, resolved to end the slaughter and went to Crete as one of the sacrificial victims. He killed the Minotaur, escaped from the maze and sailed triumphant home. Sadly, on his journey back he forgot to raise a signal to tell his father of his success. Aegeus, believing his son dead, killed himself before Theseus landed; Theseus succeeded him and is credited with founding Athenian democracy. In 1900, a historical basis for the legend emerged when British archaeologist Sir Arthur Evans discovered a vast Bronze Age palace at Knossos in Crete. Its rulers – perhaps including Minos himself – had left abundant evidence of a major bull cult, suggesting the origins of the mythical Minotaur, while the palace itself, with its maze of corridors and rooms, may well have been the original Labyrinth. Today, the bull cult endures only in Spain's bullrings.

Generations of Apis bulls were worshipped by the ancient Egyptians as manifestations on Earth of the god Ptah. Here, an Apis bull carries the mummy of a deceased notable to the Hall of Judgement.

This wall painting from Knossos, centre of the Minoan civilization of Crete, shows the famous 'bull leaping' rites, in which youths and girls performed gymnastic feats over the backs of huge, sacred bulls.

Athens sent annual tribute of human sacrifice to the Cretan Minotaur – until the hero Theseus slew the monster, as seen on this vase.

Legend tells how the god Poseidon, angry at King Minos, cursed his wife Pasiphae with unnatural love for a great bull sent by the god from the sea. She birthed the Minotaur, half man and half bull.

Europa of Tyre attracted the desire of Zeus, king of the gods. He carried her off to Crete, where he fathered on her Minos, founder of the Minoan civilization.

Zeus often took animal form to further his love affairs with mortals. To abduct Europa, he became a bull.

37

Herakles: 'Superman' of the ancient world

The Greek view of what made a god was elastic, stretching to include several mortal heroes who became demi-gods. Among them were Theseus of Athens; Perseus, who slew snake-haired Medusa the Gorgon; Jason, who led the quest for the Golden Fleece; Bellerophon, rider of the winged horse Pegasus; and Herakles (Hercules), the ancient world's 'Superman'. Son of Zeus by a mortal, Herakles was blessed with superhuman strength – but cursed with the enmity of Zeus's wife, the goddess Hera. As a baby he thwarted her first attempt on his life, strangling the snakes she sent to kill him. He grew to be a matchless warrior, and Hera struck again, inflicting on him a fit of madness in which he killed his wife and children. As penance he had to perform 12 tasks: the 'labours of Herakles'. He had to kill or capture monsters like the nine-headed Hydra and maneating Stymphalion birds, and obtain fabulous trophies. One was the girdle of Hippolyta, queen of the Amazons, a female warrior nation. She gave it him willingly, but then Hera stirred up the Amazons so that Herakles had to fight them, and kill Hippolyta. In his last task – seizing Cerberus, the underworld's three-headed guard dog – Herakles defeated Hades, king of the dead, and so won immortality. When his mortal life ended, he joined the gods and was at last reconciled with Hera – as her divine son-in-law. The Classical world honoured Herakles as a demi-god, raised temples in his name and spread his cult across the Roman Empire. Portrayed with his war club and Hera's serpents, he was also identified with several Celtic deities, including Ogmios, god of eloquence and poetry. His name appears at Romano-British shrines, and some scholars think Britain's huge, carved hill figures, like the Cerne Abbas Giant, are representations of Herakles.

The last of the 12 labours of Herakles was to abduct Cerberus, three-headed guard dog of the Underworld. His defeat of its master, Hades, king of the dead, won him immortality.

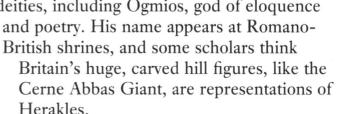

Herakles's first labour was to kill the savage Nemean lion. Finding that even magical weapons could not wound the beast, he strangled it with his bare hands.

The Cerne Abbas giant, cut into a hill in Dorset, England, may be an ancient fertility symbol. It is said to resemble a picture of Herakles found on a piece of Romano-British pottery.

Mighty Herakles prepares for combat. His mortal life ended tragically: his wife Deianira was tricked into killing him by means of a tunic smeared with the poisonous blood of an enemy.

Herakles (Hercules) remains the best known ancient hero, many times portrayed in movies. Lou Ferrigno, seen here in *Hercules* (1983), was well cast: he had formerly played the 'Incredible Hulk'.

❏ Herakles's 11th labour was to gather the golden apples of the Hesperides, garden of the gods. No mortal could go there, so Herakles sent the giant Atlas in his place – and meanwhile took over Atlas's task of supporting the world on his shoulders. Centuries later, Shakespeare's Globe Theatre in London took its name from its sign: Herakles carrying the globe of the Earth.

❏ Mad, bad Roman Emperor Commodus (161-192) made his subjects worship him as *Herakles Secundus* ('the second Herakles'). In his role of heroic warrior, he devoted his time to the arena as both fight promoter and gladiator. But his idea of amusement was to arrange fights between cripples – and the 1,000 gladiators he himself boasted of killing in the arena were allowed no weapons.

❏ Long before 'women's lib', Greek myth created the Amazons: a race of women who spurned men, using them only to sire children. Baby boys were killed, mutilated or sent to their fathers. Girls were raised as warriors, their right breasts burned off to allow freer use of weapons (Amazon: 'breastless'). The Amazons were said to have built the temple of Diana at Ephesus, one of the Wonders of the Ancient World. Sixteenth century explorers gave their name to the Amazon River because of local tales of a female warrior tribe.

39

Good versus evil – the cosmic battle

Persia (modern Iran) is a land of contrasts – mountain and valley, summer heat and winter chill – and its great prophets were inspired by another contrast: good and evil. Persia's earliest gods and demons were personified virtues and vices: Hospitality and Victory, Wrath and Procrastination. Tradition says that in c.600 B.C. (historians now favour 1500-1000 B.C.) the prophet Zoroaster (Zarathustra) adapted these to his vision of a cosmic battle between good and evil. The spirit of light and wisdom, Ahura Mazda ('Wise Lord'), became Supreme Being, Creator of all good, waging perpetual war with Ahriman ('Destructive Thought'), source of all evil. Ahura Mazda created Persia as an earthly paradise: Ahriman spoiled it by inventing heat, cold, disease and so on. Ahura Mazda urged men to virtue and heavenly rewards as 'followers of truth': Ahriman tempted them to sin – and Hell. 'Every gift I have given mankind,' said Ahura Mazda, 'has been counterbalanced by an evil present from Ahriman . . . author of unrest, misfortune and death.' But good was destined to triumph: Zoroaster's revelation of 'the Good Religion' heralded the last round of the battle, in which Ahura Mazda would triumph and the world be perfected. Later teachers expanded Zoroastrianism: one spin-off faith, Zurvanism, held that Time (Zurvan) was the ultimate Being, source of both Ahura Mazda and Ahriman. A later Persian prophet, Mani (c.A.D. 215-276), blended Zoroastrian dualism with Christianity and Buddhism. The Church condemned Manicheanism as heresy, but it lingered into the 13th century. Despite centuries of persecution, Zarathustra's teachings endure as a minority religion with some 150,000 followers, notably the Parsees of Bombay.

A Zoroastrian prays at Ahura Mazda's holy fire. He wears the *kusti* (cord, or belt) and *sudra* (shirt), sacred to all followers of Zoroaster.

Under Persia's Sassanid rulers (c.A.D. 226-641) – among them Shapur I, seen here in a carving of c.A.D. 260 – Zoroastrianism was the unifying religion of a powerful state.

A winged sun disc forms an appropriate setting for a portrayal of Ahura Mazda (sometimes called Ormazd), lord of light and wisdom. This relief carving dates from the 9th century B.C.

Envoys from conquered lands carry tribute to Persia's kings of the Achaemenid dynasty (c.500-331 B.C.): a detail from the fine carvings on their palace at Persepolis, near modern Shiraz, Iran.

❏ Zarathustra taught that Ahura Mazda created heavenly beings, the Bounteous Immortals, to aid him against evil. These figures, adapted from the older gods, inspired Christianity's Archangels.

❏ Ancient Zoroastrians held both burial of the dead and cremation to be evil inventions of Ahriman: the one polluted the Earth, the other the sacred fire. Instead, they exposed their dead on top of high towers, for disposal by vultures and the elements, as modern Parsees still do.

❏ The symbols of Zoroastrianism are the sacred cord (*kusti*) and white cotton shirt (*sudra*), worn at all times as symbolic armour in the battle against evil.

❏ Zoroastrian texts were preserved (and modified) by the Magi, Persia's priestly caste – best known to Christians in the persons of the Three Wise Men.

❏ Manicheanism hinged on the fight between the principles of Light (good) and Darkness (evil). The whole material world was evil: the soul owned sparks of light, but was trapped in darkness unless it achieved salvation by knowledge. Devotees reduced involvement with the material world by asceticism. Meat-eating was out, but fruit like cucumbers and melons held a good share of light and thus were acceptable.

Priests of the sacred grove

A popular view of Celtic religion in pre-Christian Europe relies on Roman reports of barbarous rites in forest glades spattered with human blood. Celts, said the Romans, raised no stone temples, but worshipped via natural features: water, hilltops and trees. In fact, the Celts built wooden shrines and earthworks, but their 'altars' were wells, rivers, bogs and pits, seen as channels to the gods below, which received offerings of treasure (we still drop coins in a wishing well 'for luck') and human sacrifices. Their 'temple' was the forest *nemeton* (sanctuary): a sacred grove, often of oaks; their 'priests' were Druids, whose true role is obscure because Celts held it improper to make written records of religious matters. Roman authors dwelt much on human sacrifice (a practice Rome had only recently abandoned), reporting that Druidic diviners read omens in human entrails or in a stabbed victim's death throes, and sacrificed captives by shooting them with arrows, impalement, or cramming them into huge wickerwork figures to be burned. But although the warrior Celts were headhunters and venerated severed heads, Druids dealt with more than bloodshed. They formed a living 'reference library', a store of their people's religious, legal and practical knowledge, and had advanced astronomical and calendrical skills. This aspect took the fancy of 18th century scholars, who credited Druids with a 'Natural Religion' derived from Abraham, all manner of magical skills – and the erection of pre-Celtic monuments like Stonehenge. British antiquarians like Iolo Morganwg 'revived' the Druid cult, and today modern 'Druids' claim to perpetuate ancient Celtic wisdom, performing mystic rites on Midsummer Day and other pagan festivals.

The human head played a most important part in Celtic religious beliefs and rites.

This Celtic stone head, perhaps carved for ritual purposes, was found beneath a Roman temple in Britain. The Romans may have purposely built their temple on a sacred site of the 'pagans' they despised.

An 18th century picture sums up the popular idea of a Druid: a sage uses a sickle to cut mistletoe in a sacred grove at Stonehenge, then thought a Druidic temple.

Like Stonehenge, most of Britain's 40 or more stone circles – like this one at Masham, Yorkshire – were formerly said to be Druidic temples. Most are older than Druidic rites, which perhaps began c.500 B.C.

Julius Caesar, conqueror of Britain in c.50 B.C., wrote that the Celts made human sacrifice in this way – burning their captives alive in giant wickerwork figures.

Modern Druidism (above) has attracted some notable characters. George Watson MacGregor Reid, Chief Druid of The British Circle of the Universal Bond from 1909 to 1946, stood (unsuccessfully) for both the British House of Commons and the United States Senate. Keeping up with the times, in June 1992 British Druids elected their first woman chief for 200 years: Dwina Murphy-Gibb, wife of rock star Robin Gibb.

❑ American Druidism began as a joke in 1963, when Minnesota youngsters protesting at compulsory attendance at school religious services created the Reformed Druids of North America. Some members developed the hoax movement seriously as a neo-Pagan religion, with branches like the New Reformed Druids of North America and *Ár Ndraíocht Féin* ('Our own Druidism'). By the mid-1980s the movement was on the wane, but a few American Druids still observe pagan festivals at a Stonehenge replica in Washington State.

'Axe age, sword age'

Heroism, fatalism and black humour, hallmarks of Viking society, colour Norse mythology. If classical myths are divine soap opera, Norse myths are sword-and-sorcery with a generous dash of comic strip. The gods are a motley crew to suit the needs of every individual. The practical man would worship thunder god Thor, 'Old Redbeard', a mighty brawler with his great hammer Mjöllnir. The more mystically minded turned to Odin, sinister lord of war and sorcery, who gifted his followers with elated states of mind inspiring both poetry and battle rage. His counterpart for women worshippers was fertility goddess Freyja, inspiration of seeresses and associated with *seidr*, a kind of witchcraft concerned mainly with divination. Her twin, the more earthy fertility god Freyr, looked after the crops and the marriage bed. Other gods included Mimir, the wise; Heimdall, the watcher; Njord, sea god and lord of ships; and trickster god Loki, a sinister comedian. Central to Norse myth is the belief that the gods themselves are doomed, and that Loki is fated to set in train the events leading to Ragnarok, 'twilight of the gods'. Other nations have predicted the world's end, but the Norsemen included even the gods in their Armageddon. Ragnarok will begin with Fimbul-winter, a three-year freeze when civilization collapses into war, treason, incest and fratricide: 'Axe age, sword age, shields are sundered; wind age, wolf age, before the world crumbles,' promises a 10th century Icelandic poet. Then comes battle between the gods, aided by warrior souls, against cosmic monsters – the World Serpent and the great wolf Fenrisulfr – and fire giants riding in a ship made of dead men's fingernails. But all are fated to fall in the battle, and Heaven and Earth are destroyed by fire.

In Norse mythology, the world is held by the great ash tree Yggdrasil. But the World Tree is under constant attack from cosmic beasts, like this stag, which gnaw away at it.

The name of popular god Thor lives on in Scandinavian personal names, place-names in Scandinavia and England – and, of course, in Thursday.

Odin will lead the gods to battle at Ragnarok, his raven on his shoulder and his spear Gungnir in his hand. But he is doomed – to be devoured by monstrous wolf Fenrisulfr.

Small bronze statuette of Freyr ('Lord'). The fertility god, with his twin sister Freya ('Lady'), belonged to a group of gods called the Vanir, said to predate Odin, Thor and the rest (the Aesir).

❏ In a Swedish fertility rite in autumn a wagon carried Freyr's image, with a priestess, the god's 'wife', round the land to bless the fields. An Icelandic saga says when Norwegian exile Gunnar Helming fled to Sweden, he used this ritual to his advantage, stealing the idol's clothes and impersonating Freyr. His performance was a hit: locals were impressed by a god who joined in their feasts, and preferred offerings of goods and money to human sacrifices – and even more impressed when Freyr's 'wife' became pregnant. Gunnar returned to Norway a rich, married man.

❏ A crude and richly comic story tells how Loki's tricks were punished when he was raped by a stallion. But the story has a sting in its tail. The progeny of the monstrous mating were Sleipnir, Odin's eight-legged horse (above); Hel, dread goddess of the underworld; Jormungandr, the World Serpent which will emerge from the seas with poisonous floods at Ragnarok; and Fenrisulfr, the destroying wolf destined to cause the death of Odin himself.

Arthur: once and future king

Arthur fights a giant in this 16th century woodcut. The Virgin Mary watches over him: Welsh tradition says he carried her image into battle, probably painted on his shield.

The story of King Arthur, Britain's legendary hero, has inspired his countrymen for 14 centuries. Welsh warriors of the Dark Ages strove to match his victories; Tudor kings justified their claim to the English throne by faking descent from him; and writers from the 9th to the 20th centuries have created libraries of 'Arthurian' literature. The Arthur of popular fantasy is king of a medieval-style court and leader of the Round Table of knights who, like modern comic strip heroes, roam the land righting wrongs. Among the best-known tales are the tragic love affair between Arthur's faithless queen Guinevere and his best knight Lancelot; and of the Quest for the Holy Grail (a chalice holding drops of Christ's blood). All this is fiction, the work of medieval romancers (some not even British: Lancelot is a French creation). But most scholars agree Arthur existed – not as a king, but a 6th century guerrilla fighter against Saxon invaders. He may have not even have been named Arthur: early chroniclers call him only *dux bellorum*, 'battle leader'. The myth-makers not only crowned him but made him immortal: the 'once and future king' who sleeps with his men in a hollow hill and will return in his country's hour of need. Storytellers transformed his military base (some Celtic hill fort) into the sophisticated court of Camelot, and the patchwork of petty Dark Age kingdoms into a glorious land called England, Logres, or 'the adventurous kingdom'. Here the mythical Arthur ruled an idealized world of chivalry, peopled with knights errrant busy with wars, tournaments, and quests in search of holy relics or damsels in distress. In this glorified form the theme of Arthur and his court became a national epic renowned as the 'Matter of Britain'.

The Round Table at Winchester is a famous fake 'Arthurian' relic from medieval times. Legend says Arthur made his table round to give each knight a seat of equal status.

❏ Arthur's legendary mounted knights may have some basis in fact. 6th century Britons fought mainly on foot or from chariots: native ponies were not up to warriors' weight. But early historians credit Arthur with battles so farflung as to suggest he may have introduced cavalry. Perhaps novelist Alfred Duggan was right: his fictional Arthur is a rustler who steals the necessary war-horses from the departing Romans.

❏ The promise that Arthur would return was taken seriously. Some claimed Philip II of Spain was only permitted to wed Britain's Queen Mary Tudor in 1554 on condition he swore to resign the kingdom to Arthur if necessary.

❏ Camelot was invented by a 12th century French poet, but that did not discourage a quest for Arthur's base. Most of Britain's major ruins, from Caerleon's Roman fortress to Tintagel's Celtic monastery, have staked a claim. From 1542 the favourite has been the 5th century hillfort of Cadbury, Somerset (above). Local legend said Arthur and his men slept under the hill — and excavations in 1966-70 showed it had been a major military base in Arthur's supposed time.

Legend says Arthur was born here at Tintagel Castle, Cornwall. But these dramatic ruins mark the site not of a castle, but a monastery.

A 19th century Arthur shown as an idealized, noble youth; a far cry from the guerrilla of history's 'Dark Ages'.

The Holy Grail perhaps began as the sacred cauldron of pagan Celtic religion, but is now firmly Christianized.

Shinto: way of the gods

S hinto (Chinese: 'divine way'; the Japanese is *Kami-no-Michi*, 'way of the gods'), Japan's ancient faith, originated in worship of divine spirits (*kami*) in natural objects or forces – mountains, trees, winds and the like. Of more than 8,000,000 *kami*, the greatest is the sun goddess Amaterasu.

Japan, says Shinto myth, was the world's first nation, born of sexual intercourse between gods (the afterbirth formed other nations). Amaterasu's grandson Ninigi came to Earth, where his great-grandson Jimmu Tenno (*Tenno*: Emperor) became first ruler of a united Japan in 660 B.C. From Jimmu the Imperial rulers, who are both gods and men, descend in an unbroken line through 125 generations to Emperor Akihito (b.1933). For centuries Buddhism was Japan's more vital faith, but after Emperor Meiji's restoration of Imperial power in 1867 Shinto was seen as a more valuable tool of nationalism.

Kokutai (State) Shinto was decreed to be not a religion but a 'national ethic' to which all must subscribe. It taught absolute dedication to Emperor and nation (as one and the same thing). In c.1937-45 Kokutai Shinto inspired Japan's wars of conquest – even led some soldiers, survivors of isolated Pacific garrisons, to fight on into the 1970s. In 1945 Allied occupation authorities forbade Kokutai Shinto and Emperor Hirohito renounced his godhead. Today, Shinto is a loosely linked organization of more than 80,000 shrines. But its most sacred objects remain the mirror, sword and jewels associated with Amaterasu; Tokyo's Meiji Shrine and Ise Shrine, near Kyoto, traditional centres of the Imperial cult, remain its major sanctuaries; and on his accession in 1989 Emperor Akihito revived an ancient ceremony of 'sleeping with the goddess' (he kept an all-night vigil in a Shinto shrine) which some allege was a step towards reaffirming his divinity.

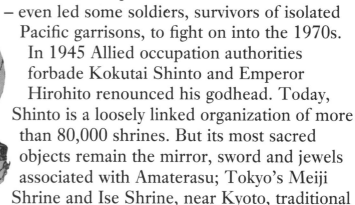

The magnificent Todai-ji Temple at Nara, Japan, where ancient Buddhist and Shinto shrines stand together, emblematic of the close ties between the two faiths.

Seen here in a 15th century print, sun goddess Amaterasu is the greatest of the many Shinto deities, and is claimed to be the ancestress of Japan's Imperial line.

State Shinto helped inspire some Japanese soldiers, like Shoichi Yokoi, seen here after capture on Guam, Marianas, in 1972, to fight on for many years after the end of World War II.

Shinto's sacred mountain, Fujiyama, an extinct volcanic peak near Tokyo, is said to be the home of the ancient creator god Kunitokotachi.

Lord Jaguar and the Long Count

From ancient times until European conquest in the 16th century, Central America saw a succession of priest-ridden societies whose subjugation to fierce gods produced a strange blend of primitive and sophisticated culture. They failed to develop wheeled vehicles, but in the service of the gods they evolved writing, astronomy and advanced maths. They built pyramidal, stone temples in cult centres so vast that Western explorers thought them cities. Their gods demanded not only conventional worship but also human sacrifice. This rite the Aztecs took to its limits: 15,000 men a year were shot with arrows, flayed, decapitated, burned, or had their hearts cut from their living bodies. Priests and worshippers did not spare themselves, but offered their own blood from pierced tongues or ears. The gods who demanded such service were often portrayed as part wild animal: above all, the jaguar, the Americas' most striking great predator, became a living image of divine power. Its worship began with the Olmecs – termed 'jaguar psychotics' by a modern zoologist. Their temples are dominated by jaguar mosaics, masks, thrones and 'were-jaguars', figures part human, part jaguar. They even moulded their babies' heads to resemble the jaguar's flattened skull. Later cultures, the Zapotecs and Maya, also knew the jaguar god. But the Maya shifted the emphasis from religious rituals to the calendar developed to schedule them. Their obsession with the measurement of time produced the Long Count calendar: a mathematical and astronomical masterpiece, covering not only days of the year but vast cycles of years within an infinity of time. It was so precise its computation of the solar year differs by no more than 0.0008 of a day from modern reckoning.

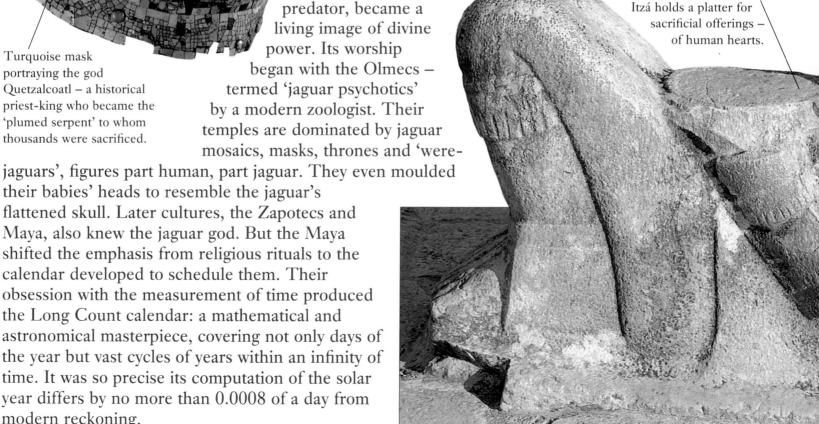

Turquoise mask portraying the god Quetzalcoatl – a historical priest-king who became the 'plumed serpent' to whom thousands were sacrificed.

A massive reclining figure at the Temple of Warriors in Chichén Itzá holds a platter for sacrificial offerings – of human hearts.

A pyramid temple at the great Mayan centre of Chichén Itzá.

Even the stairs honour the Long Count. Four great staircases total 364 steps: the platform makes 365 – the number of days in the year.

Such altar-statues, or *Chac Mools*, were used by both Toltecs and Maya.

Mayan gods demanded endless blood sacrifice. In this carving of c.750 A.D. a worshipper makes an offering of his blood by drawing cactus spines through his tongue.

Golden hoard and 'green hell'

The Inca Empire in the Andean region of South America was destroyed in the 1530s by gold-hungry Spanish conquerors. From survivors of their massacres they learned of El Dorado (Spanish: 'the Gilded'), variously interpreted as a 'Golden City' or a 'Golden Man'. For many years European expeditions sought El Dorado throughout South America, not knowing the Spaniards had probably destroyed it (or him) in 1536, when they looted the Chibcha people of Bolivia. The Sun-worshipping Chibcha revered gold as 'sweat of the Sun', and every year their chief, coated in gold dust, led his people in a sacrifice in which gold and jewels were thrown into Lake Guatavita (near modern Bogotá). Although they did not recognize this rite as the true source of the El Dorado legend, the Spaniards learned of the lake – and killed thousands of Indian slaves in attempts to drain it. More modern, less greedy Europeans sought the lost cities of the Incas – and one, British explorer Colonel Percy Fawcett (1867-?1925), sought the Incas themselves. Fawcett had spent many years in the Mato Grosso, the vast Amazon jungle – 'I love that green hell,' he wrote – and believed it concealed vast ruined cities where lost remnants of the Inca peoples still lived. From an account supposedly written by a Portuguese explorer in 1753 Fawcett learned of 'City X' deep in the Mato Grosso, and in 1925 set out with two other Europeans to find it. They disappeared, but for decades travellers told of meeting an old European wandering the jungle, or of encountering forest Indians who claimed to have killed Fawcett's party – or who said he had found 'City X' and stayed there as a chief. Irish medium Geraldine Cummins claimed to be in clairvoyant contact with Fawcett from 1935, when he told her he had found an 'Atlantean settlement', until his death in 1948.

A gold and turquoise god of the Chimu civilization, which flourished in north Peru and the Andes from c.A.D. 1000.

The figure's base forms the blade of a ceremonial knife. The Incas, who conquered the Chimu in c.1470, valued such work for its beauty – the later Spanish conquerors loved its gold.

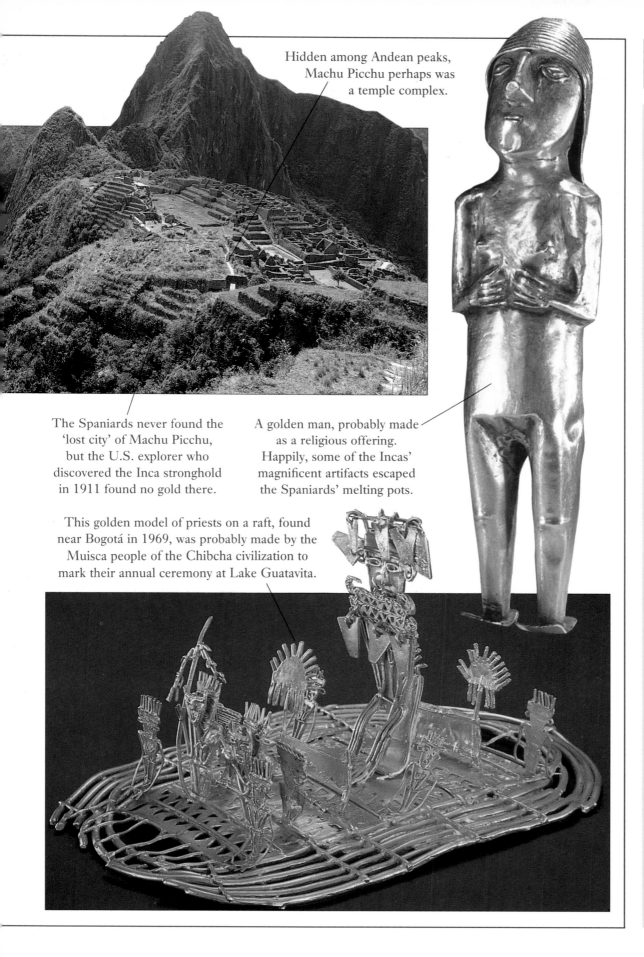

Hidden among Andean peaks, Machu Picchu perhaps was a temple complex.

The Spaniards never found the 'lost city' of Machu Picchu, but the U.S. explorer who discovered the Inca stronghold in 1911 found no gold there.

A golden man, probably made as a religious offering. Happily, some of the Incas' magnificent artifacts escaped the Spaniards' melting pots.

This golden model of priests on a raft, found near Bogotá in 1969, was probably made by the Muisca people of the Chibcha civilization to mark their annual ceremony at Lake Guatavita.

Native American dreamers and dancers

Today conservationists contrast white settlers' misuse of North America's natural resources with the 'green' approach of Native Americans, whose religious beliefs taught respect for nature. The Great Spirit was present in all things: animals were seen as the original owners of the land and the ancestors of both modern animals and humans. Protective spirits or demi-gods included many animals, like Raven and Blue Jay, as well as the Sun, thunder, maize and flint. Evil spirits also abounded and must be pacified by special rites. 'Medicine men' – visionaries who could enter the spirit world in trance state – mediated between humanity and the spirit world. But spirit visions were not reserved to these shamans alone: adolescent boys underwent solitary fasts to contact the guardian spirits who would give them their adult name; war leaders sought guidance in prophetic dreams. Rituals often took the form of mass dances, many lasting for days. Plains Indians held a Sun Dance each year to ensure the renewal of nature. In its mildest form it was a test of endurance: braves danced for days round a sacred tree, without sleep or food. Some tribes, like the Cheyenne, extended this self-torture: dancers had skewers thrust into their chests, which were tied to the tree, and danced backwards till their flesh tore through. In the 1880s another ritual dance arose when Wovoka, a Paiute, had a vision of the end of the 'white man's world' and of a Native American saviour who would then establish an earthly paradise. His followers gained ecstatic glimpses of the promised utopia in the frenzied 'Ghost Dance'. When white officials fearing unrest sent troops to suppress the dances, the Sioux rose. The 'Messiah War', last major Indian War, ended with the infamous massacre of the Sioux at Wounded Knee in December 1890.

Demi-god Raven presides over a totem pole, erected to honour the dead, and carved with animal spirits linked with the dead man's ancestors.

❏ After the collapse of the Ghost Dance movement came the cult known as the Peyote Road. Some Native American peoples had long obtained visions by chewing the hallucinatory peyote cactus. In the 1890s Quanah Parker, half-Comanche war leader, expanded this practice into a whole new religion which led to the foundation in 1918 of the Native American Church – a mixture of Christian beliefs and practices with the sacramental use of peyote. By the 1930s it was estimated that about half the Native American population of the U.S.A. belonged to this church, which retains its importance today.

Paintings cover the rock face at Newspaper Rock, Utah. The image of the mounted huntsman shooting a stag is an example of sympathetic magic: the artist painted a successful hunt to make it happen.

The horned figure represents the shaman or medicine man, who acts as a living bridge between the worlds of spirits and humans.

Warriors act out sighting an enemy in the 'Discovery Dance'. Special dances attended every important aspect of life, as rituals to bring guidance and success.

Today Native Americans, like this modern Narraganset medicine man in his traditional regalia, seek to preserve their ancestors' knowledge and customs.

Shamans of the north

One of the oldest surviving religious traditions is the shamanism of northern Europe and Asia, which may date back to the Stone Age. From North America to Finland and Siberia, shaman cultures believe in a spirit world separate from but affecting that of humans. Disharmony between the worlds causes human troubles, from famine to individual illness. Only the shaman – a figure between priest and 'witch doctor' – can enter both worlds and restore the balance between them. Aided by ritual dancing and drumming, meditation, or hallucinatory drugs, he or she enters a trance state in which the soul leaves the body and travels to the Otherworld for spirit guidance. The shaman is a seer, with prophetic skills; a 'social worker' who seeks spiritual reasons and remedies for his community's problems; and above all a spiritual healer. To become a shaman requires both a divine call and a rigorous apprenticeship, culminating in an ordeal of symbolic death, dismemberment and rebirth. This passage through death equips the soul to visit the upperworld of spirits and the underworld where the souls of the sick await rescue. The shaman is guided in his journeys by a totemic spirit, sometimes an ancestor but often an animal. An Inuit shaman whose totem was the wolf-being Amarok said he became kin to wolves as a 5-year-old, when his father took him to a wolf den where for 24 hours he played unharmed among the beasts. He claimed to understand wolf 'language' – and staggered a Canadian zoologist with 'translations' of howls (as inter-wolf reports on the movements of both prey animals and men) which events proved correct. Such close contact with the animal world enables shamans to guide hunters, ensuring food for the people.

Siberian shaman in impressive traditional costume, with his 'medicine bag' of amulets and his indispensable sacred drum.

The shaman's drum, made of hide and decorated with magic symbols. It is the key with which he unlocks the door to the spirit world, beating on it with a spoon-shaped drumstick until he falls into a trance, aided by hallucinatory drugs.

The magic drum is common to all shaman cultures. This is an Inuit example, made of hide and wood, from the Northwest coast of America

Dressed in animal skins, horned and tailed, the shaman enters the animal kingdom in spirit. The spirit hunt he carries out enables his people to carry out a successful hunt in the flesh.

By ritual dancing and drumming these Yakut shamans from eastern Russia seek to free their spirits from their bodies to enter the spirit world or realm of the dead.

FACT FILE

❏ The Inuit of Alaska say human sins form dirt in the spirit world. This clogs the hair of the Sea Woman, angering her into a refusal to give mortals her seals, walruses and whales. To save the people from starving, the shaman's spirit must go under the sea to comb the Sea Woman's hair clean. Only then will she give good hunting.

❏ The Vikings' *völva*, or seeress, derived from shaman tradition. A Norse saga describes how the *völva* was consulted. Clad in animal skins (including calfskin boots and catskin gloves), she ate ritually of animal hearts before entering trance, while a helper summoned the spirits with song. Then she reported what the spirits had told her.

❏ In Mongolia, land of horsemen, the shaman's horse was not, as we might expect, the best mount available. Burials reveal that many were lame – crippled with arthritis. They may have been kept into old age because of special markings. But some authorities think their lameness was not the effect of age, but the identifying factor of a shaman horse, related to the ritual deformity of the Lame King of some mystic cults.

❏ Many shamanistic cultures believe both mortal and spirit realms are supported by a vast World Tree. Sometimes the shaman's drum is said to be made from its wood.

Dreaming down under

The first Europeans to study the Aboriginal peoples of Australia concluded they had no religion at all – and the Aborigines were equally shocked by what they saw as the irreligious attitude of European Christians. The Europeans had failed to see the wood for the trees: native Australian religious belief is so closely interwoven with daily life and social structure that the newcomers simply could not distinguish it. Where many faiths look to the future, in a life after death, Aboriginal belief looks back to the time of creation: the 'Dreamtime'. In that age ancestor spirits such as kangaroo-men and bowerbird-women lived on Earth. They shaped its hills, rocks, waterholes and trees; created humans; and taught them how to live on and with the land. So to the Aborigines the entire land is a 'temple'; the priesthoods of other faiths are replaced by a tradition in which everyone is an equal inheritor of religious knowledge; and living by the moral laws of the ancestor spirits is the major part of worship. Those who break these laws may be literally cursed to death by 'pointing the bone'. The executioner prepares a sharpened bone (or stick) and 'loads' it with psychic energy before pointing it at the condemned man. The victim is now regarded by his people as dead – and his own belief in the ritual ensures his death within a few days. Dreamtime laws and legends are passed on through generations by song-cycles, and are re-enacted in song and dance at 'corroboree' ceremonies. At other times people may go 'walkabout' as pilgrims to sacred landmarks associated with Dreamtime events, guided by 'Songlines', a psychic map accessed through ancestral chants. Today the modern world has broken down much of the Aborigines' traditions and their link with the land; yet a few groups strive to preserve their ancient values, beliefs and ceremonies.

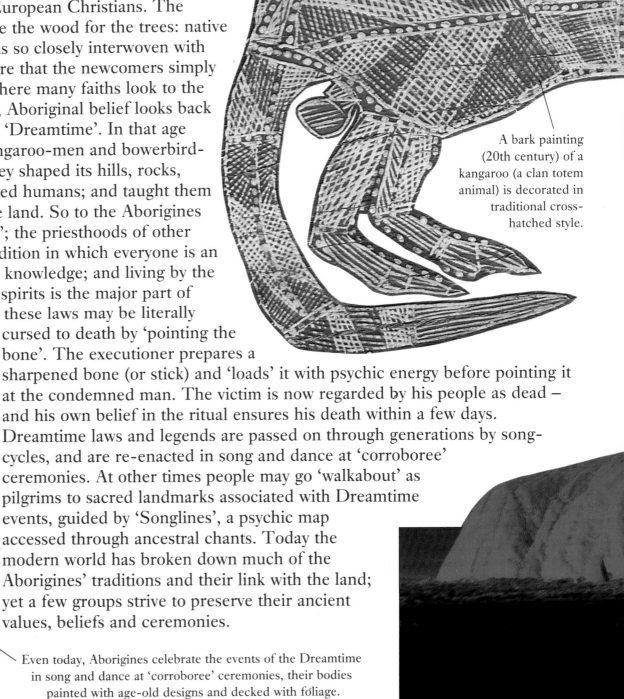

A bark painting (20th century) of a kangaroo (a clan totem animal) is decorated in traditional cross-hatched style.

Even today, Aborigines celebrate the events of the Dreamtime in song and dance at 'corroboree' ceremonies, their bodies painted with age-old designs and decked with foliage.

This bark painting depicts a Creation myth. Both people and animals share ancestor-beings who were part animal, part human.

Aborigines honour the spirit shared by the kangaroo-men's issue, human and animal alike.

Bark paintings – an art-form unique to the Aborigines – not only have ritual significance but form teaching aids by which elders explain tribal myths to the next generation.

The whole landscape is a memorial to and a living link with the events of the Dreamtime, and landmarks like mighty Ayers Rock are sacred sites to this day.

❏ Since 1969 Alan Webb has been one of the few Aborigines to survive the curse of 'pointing the bone'. An Australian court cleared him of manslaughter charges, ruling his killing of a fellow tribesman acidental, but tribal elders disagreed and condemned him to death. Despite Webb's 'white' lifestyle, he believed implicitly that he would die once the killing-bone pointed at him. So he fled and began a life on the run. Years later, his would-be executioners were still trying to find him so they could point the bone.

❏ Binbinga Aborigines tell how, back in the Dreamtime, humans were unable to catch the large bats (flying foxes) which had been provided for them to eat. Snake ancestor-spirit Bobbi-Bobbi came to the rescue. He tore out one of his own ribs to make a throwing weapon – and thus invented the boomerang (below).

Killers for faith: Assassins and Thugs

Appearing in the terrifying form of Durga (Devi), wife of Shiva, Hindu goddess Kali, patroness of the Thugs, wears a necklace of skulls and a belt of severed heads.

The word 'assassin' dates from the 12th century. It is from *hashishiyun* ('hashish smokers'), Arabic name of a Muslim sect founded in c.1090 by Hasan ibn Sabbah (c.1033-1124), called the 'Old Man of the Mountain' from his fortress at Alamut in the Elburz Mountains of Iran. He sent suicide squads, inspired by visions of Paradise gained by smoking hashish and promised eternal bliss if they died in action, to cut down opponents of his heretical sect – orthodox Muslims and Christians. He claimed 70,000 followers, including his killer élite the *fedayeen* ('devoted ones'; a name still used by Muslim extremists), linked by a 'magical' intelligence network: an early 'pigeon post'. The Assassins' reign of terror in the Middle East ended after 1256, when Mongol conqueror Hulagu took Alamut – but legend says some Assassins escaped to India, to become worshippers of the Hindu goddess Kali, the 'Black Mother', and establish the caste of hereditary murderers called Thugs (Hindi *thag*: 'Deceiver') or *Phansigars* ('Stranglers'). Certainly, Hindus and Muslims were united in Thuggee – but Hindu tradition traces the cult back to c.800 A.D. Thugs are said to have killed c.1,000,000 persons in central India in the 17th-19th centuries. They operated in gangs up to 150 strong. *Belhals* (spies) located parties of travellers; *bhartotes* (killers) ambushed and murdered them by strangling with a *rumal* (kerchief); *lughahs* (diggers) gutted and dismembered the bodies, using a sacred pickaxe ('Kali's tooth'), then buried them. In c.1800-45 Thuggee was stamped out by India's British rulers. Sir William Sleeman (1788-1856) masterminded a 'hearts and minds' campaign to turn Indian villagers against the Thugs and recruited undercover agents to hunt them down.

Thugs carry off the bodies of murdered travellers for ritual mutilation and burial in a remote place.

The *rumal* (kerchief; strip of twisted cloth) with which a victim has been strangled is still tight around his neck.

The Hindu goddess Lakshmi, as benevolent as Kali is terrible, rides with her husband, the powerful Vishnu, on Garuda, king of all birds.

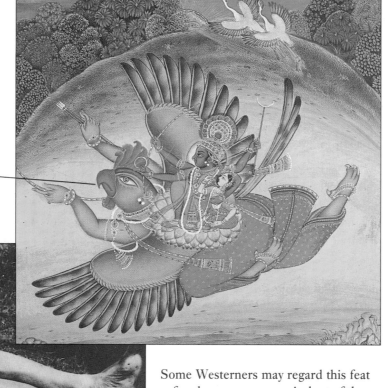

Some Westerners may regard this feat of endurance as an equivalent of the 'rope trick', but this devotee of Kali is lying on a bed of nails as a penance, to humble himself at one of the goddess's shrines.

Ancient wisdom of Africa

The traditional beliefs of Africa, vast cradle of the human race, are as various as its peoples. Most have in common a deep belief in the spirit world, whether the spirits venerated are those of ancestors, natural forces, or totem animals. Many peoples, like the Zulu of South Africa, also believe in a 'great spirit', whom the Zulu call simply Unkulunkulu ('the Chief'). In the past, most white settlers scorned African peoples' beliefs and dismissed their priests, prophets and healers as 'witch doctors'. Now it is acknowledged that Africa's ancient wisdom, in particular the herbal lore of its healers, has much to offer. Although most black Africans now profess Christianity or Islam, traditional beliefs retain their hold. This is not always for the good: in internal wars in modern times, rebel leaders have enlisted 'witches' to terrorize peaceful villagers into supporting them (as did the Mau Mau in Kenya in the 1950s), or to persuade their troops that fetishes (charms) or 'magic potions' could make them bullet-proof. The Simba guerrillas in the Congo (Zaire) in the 1960s believed this, and were massacred by white mercenaries. In the 1970s tyrants like 'Field Marshal' Idi Amin of Uganda and 'Emperor' Bokassa of the Central African Republic buttressed their power by exploiting their peoples' traditional beliefs. In the 16th-19th centuries native West African beliefs were 'exported' via the slave trade. Some melded with the Christianity forced on the slaves to form new faiths – among which at least two still have many followers. The Voodoo of the Caribbean islands blends African magical lore with Roman Catholicism. The Macumba cults of Brazil unite rites originating with the West African Yoruba people with both Spiritualism and older European cults, including white and black magic.

Ashanti craftsmen (Asante; modern Ghana) carved fetish figures like this 'antelope man' for religious purposes. They are still sometimes used in fertility ceremonies.

A Nigerian healer at work: his medicine is in a water buck's horn lying across the patient's afflicted part. Such traditional healers were once dismissed as 'witch doctors'.

Although, like other black African peoples, many Zulu of South Africa are now nominally Christian, the *sangoma* (shaman) still plays a part in their traditional way of life.

Long hair braided with beads into the style known as 'dreadlocks' (and now mainly associated with West Indian Rastafarians) is also a mark of distinction among the Zulu people.

Voodoo worshippers in Haiti seek to call up a spirit. Voodoo blends traditional West African beliefs with Christianity. Its name is said to come from an African word for a spirit: *voudou*.

Miracle men of Tibet

Most Eastern religions teach believers to look inward and cultivate in themselves the powers of the mind. Yogis (holy men) strive to school the mind to master the body, thus achieving such supernormal powers as levitation, telepathy and (by controlling the metabolism to produce 'suspended animation') the ability to survive long periods of living burial. An especially mystical form of Buddhism evolved in Tibet, cut off from the outside world by the Himalaya. Tibetan lamas (holy men) seek enlightenment through spiritual exercises that include prolonged contemplation of religious symbols (mandalas) and endless repetition of words or phrases (mantras). Their 'creative visualization' is said to endow them with the powers of teleportation (moving themselves or objects from place to place by mind power); invisibility; producing *tulpas* (creatures of their thoughts that become 'real' beings); and *tumo* (control of body heat that enables the adept to endure long periods of naked contemplation in the Himalayan snows). Tibetan Buddhism was little known in the West until the later 19th century, when travellers' tales of lamas' amazing feats attracted much attention – and inspired some Western mystics to incorporate 'Tibetan' elements into their creeds. Notable was Russian-American Helena Petrovna Blavatsky (1831-91), whose worldwide travels included Tibet. In New York in the 1870s she founded a cult called Theosophy, which she claimed was based on spirit guidance from 'Hidden Masters' in Tibet. Blavatsky was denounced as a fraud by the Society for Psychical Research and others, but Theosophy flourished especially in India, where Mahatma Gandhi is said to have been influenced by it. Many Westerners have since adopted outward forms of 'Eastern wisdom' – from yoga exercises to incense sticks.

A bronze figure of Tara, the great goddess of Tibetan Buddhism. Like her husband, the *bodhisattva* (Buddhist saint) Avalokitesvara, she is seen as a saviour, a deity full of love and compassion.

The Potala, palace of the exiled Dalai Lama, at Lhasa, Tibet. Legend says secret tunnels link it to Chang Shambhala, an earthly paradise like the fictional 'Shangri-La'.

Lord Mara, chief tempter of the Buddha and arch-demon of Buddhist theology, is the enemy of all who seek *nirvana* (supreme enlightenment).

Mara holds the Tibetan 'Wheel of Life'. Its six 'palaces' symbolize the cycle of death and rebirth, and the temptations along the way.

Although Lamaism, the Tibetan form of Buddhism, has been persecuted since the Chinese invasion of 1950, some monks are still able to pursue lives of prayer and contemplation.

FACT FILE

❏ Exiled from Tibet since the Chinese takeover in 1950, the present Dalai Lama, Tenzin Gyatso (b.1935) (below), 14th reincarnation of the first holy man to hold the office of Tibetan 'priest-king' in the 17th century, has suggested that he may also be the last in the line; that he himself will not be reincarnated.

❏ In the 1960s 'hippies' seeking enlightenment sometimes tried trepanation: a hole is drilled in the skull and, in theory, lets in more oxygen to 'expand the brain'. It was popularized in the bestselling books of 'Tibetan lama' T. Lobsang Rampa (in fact, an English handyman who never visited Tibet), who claimed he had undergone the operation to 'open a third eye'. The present author saw a hippie trepanation done – in a bar, with a mallet and a six-inch nail, the 'patient' having been anaesthetized with several pints of rough cider.

The man who talked with Angels

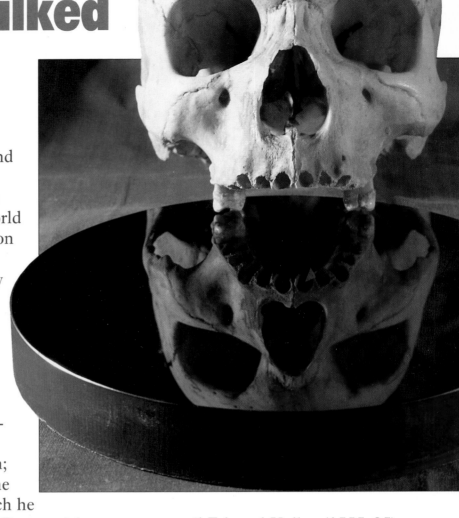

In the England of John Dee (1527-1608) most people saw little difference between science and magic. Dee was among the best astronomers, mathematicians and geographers of the time; his map-making won him the friendship of New World explorer Sir Walter Raleigh. But he was looked on as a magician – and regarded himself as one, devoting as much effort to alchemy and astrology as to conventional learning. As an astrologer he was consulted in turn by King Edward VI (1537-53) and Queen Mary I (1516-58), but was accused of plotting the latter's death by magic when he cast a favourable horoscope for her then imprisoned half-sister Elizabeth. On 'Bloody Mary's' death, Queen Elizabeth I (1533-1603) made Dee her Astrologer Royal. He was often sent abroad: officially on scientific research; secretly as a spy for the Admiralty. On one trip he acquired a 'scrying glass': a magic mirror in which he expected to see visions. But no visions came – until Edward Kelley (1555-95) offered himself as a medium. Kelley, whose ears had been lopped as punishment for forgery, had a foul reputation as a necromancer (one who works magic through corpses). But when he claimed that Angels spoke to him through the mirror in the 'Enochian language' of Heaven, Dee believed him. The two toured Europe, where noblemen entertained them royally – until they realized the angelic messages never seemed to be of practical use. A seven-year partnership ended when Dee married a young and pretty wife – and Kelley announced that the Angels commanded a wife swap. Kelley stayed abroad, where he died in an attempted jail break in Prague. Dee went home to England, where at last only a lonely, poverty stricken death saved him from facing charges of sorcery under witch-hunting King James I.

Painted at the age of 67, Dr. John Dee seems in pensive mood, perhaps regretting the trouble his reputation as a magician brought him.

Dee and Kelley probably used a disc of polished obsidian (black glass) like this as a 'scrying glass'. Gazing long into the reflective surface concentrates the seer's spiritual powers.

Protected by a 'magic circle', necromancers raise from a grave at Walton-le-Dale, Lancashire, the corpse of a man believed to have left a concealed treasure.

Edward Kelley conjures with spell book and staff in an 18th century print of one of the foul deeds attributed to him.

A hard-headed ruler and reputed the intellectual equal of most men of her time, Queen Elizabeth I of England nevertheless appointed Dee as her 'Royal Astrologer'.

FACT FILE

❏ Dee's 'scrying glass' was described at the time as being of polished obsidian (black volcanic glass) and was said to be an Aztec artifact looted from the New World by Spanish conqueror Hernando Cortés in the 1520s. The British Museum, London, now displays a sphere of pinkish crystal which is sometimes identified as the magic mirror, although by other accounts this sphere was given to Dee by Uriel, Angel of light.

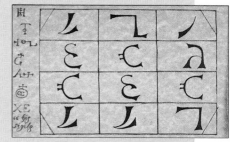

❏ Say *'Ils d ialprt, soba upaah chis nanba zixlay dodsih,'* and you might have a heavenly visitor. It is a bidding call in the 'Enochian language' (from the patriarch Enoch, who, according to some divines' interpretations of the *Book of Genesis*, was bodily taken up to Heaven) used by Kelley and Dee, who tried to codify it (above), to talk with Angels.

❏ Some say Dee was the model for Shakespeare's 'Prospero' in *The Tempest*. It is more likely that mighty magician was based on physician and astrologer Simon Forman (1552-1611), whom several associates of Shakespeare are known to have consulted.

The witches of the West

Two 'witches' were hanged in 1618 for killing by magic Henry, son of the Earl of Rutland, whose image stands on the 'witchcraft tomb' at Bottesford, Leicestershire.

Witches appear in Egyptian papyri, Greek myth and the Old Testament, but Western Europe's great 'witch craze' did not occur until comparatively modern times. On witchcraft, people in the so-called 'Dark Ages' (c.A.D. 500-1000) were more enlightened than their descendants. In the 9th century the Church forbade belief in witchcraft – but not its practice, because, great theologians said, that did not exist. But from the 14th century Church and State began to equate heresy (religious unorthodoxy) with witchcraft. Catholic and, later, Protestant authorities saw witchcraft as a great conspiracy to win Europe for Satan. This was partly an expression of the Churches' traditional anti-feminism: most accused witches were women – some, like Joan of Arc (considered both witch and heretic), women whose refusal to conform to traditional stereotypes made them political and social undesirables. In the witchhunters' heyday, the 16th-17th centuries, it was generally believed that witches regularly anointed themselves with 'devil's grease' that enabled them to fly to Sabbats (meetings) where they had sex with demons and worshipped Satan (who appeared as a giant goat or toad) with obscene rites. In fact, the great majority of those who confessed (often under torture) to witchcraft were 'drop outs' who were made scapegoats for sudden misfortunes, from crop failure to plague – or persons suffering from religious mania. Modern 'witches' (see later pages) claim as many as 500,000 witches were judicially burned or hanged: the true figure may be nearer 30,000. At Bamberg, Germany, notorious as Europe's centre of witch hunting, only c.900 trials were held in c.1610-35, when the mania was at its height. A witch was legally burned at Glarus, Switzerland, in 1782 – but by that time the scientific rationalism of the 18th century had ended the witch craze.

A great horned goat – the Evil One himself – presides at 'The Witches Sabbath' nightmarishly portrayed by Spanish artist Francisco Goya (1746-1828).

Some of England's 'Lancashire Witches', tried in 1612, are seen in a print of the time. 20 persons were accused: 8 women and 2 men were hanged.

A demon, supposedly the 'familiar' servant granted to witches by Satan, flies in formation with a male and female witch as they ride the wind on broomsticks.

The five-pointed star called a pentagram is one of the most powerful symbols used in magical rituals. Witches were said to use it reversed – single point downward.

❑ The word Sabbat perhaps did not derive from the Hebrew word for the 'seventh [holy] day' (as anti-Semites liked to believe), but from the French *s'esbettre*, 'to fling oneself about', a reference to the witches' orgiastic revels.

❑ 17th century witch hunters said witches had 'international conference centres' where they held huge Sabbats on such major festivals as Walpurgis Night (April 30; also called Beltane) and All Hallows Eve (October 31; Halloween). Among the most important were the Brocken peak in Germany's Harz Mountains; the Blåkulla plain in Sweden; and La Hendaye, southwest France – where 12,000 witches were said to gather.

❑ If the same authorities are right, English witches were the best fed. At the Sabbat, they said, German witches feasted on sliced turnips cut to resemble the sacred Host; French witches on the flesh of infants; Spanish witches on stolen corpses; Swiss witches on bat stew. But English witches had roast beef and ale.

❑ All witch hunters agreed witches had sex with Satan – but via incubi (male demons) for women, and succubi (female demons) for men. For women the act was not pleasant: Satan's member was scaly and spiky (sometimes forked) and his semen (stolen from human corpses) was said to be icy cold.

Matthew Hopkins, 'Witchfinder General'

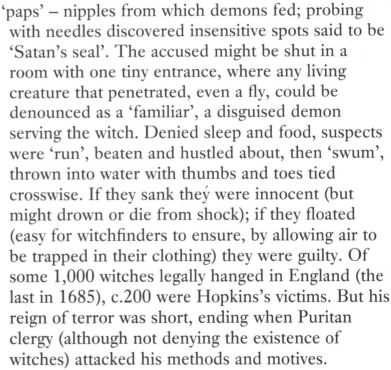

England's Civil War (1642-51), in part a religious conflict between Puritan Parliamentarians and 'high church' Royalists, saw the nation's major witch scare and its most infamous witch hunter. In 1644 lawyer Matthew Hopkins alleged that witches at Manningtree, Essex, had sent a demon in the shape of a bear to attack him. He had 29 persons arrested: 4 were hanged – others perhaps bribed him to drop charges. Scenting riches, Hopkins styled himself 'Witchfinder General'. He toured Puritan Eastern England, exposing witches for c.£20 (then some two years' pay for a labourer) per conviction – plus generous expenses. Most of his victims were old, poor men and women, bullied into confessions by Hopkins and his 'searchers'. Moles and blemishes on suspects' bodies were declared 'paps' – nipples from which demons fed; probing with needles discovered insensitive spots said to be 'Satan's seal'. The accused might be shut in a room with one tiny entrance, where any living creature that penetrated, even a fly, could be denounced as a 'familiar', a disguised demon serving the witch. Denied sleep and food, suspects were 'run', beaten and hustled about, then 'swum', thrown into water with thumbs and toes tied crosswise. If they sank they were innocent (but might drown or die from shock); if they floated (easy for witchfinders to ensure, by allowing air to be trapped in their clothing) they were guilty. Of some 1,000 witches legally hanged in England (the last in 1685), c.200 were Hopkins's victims. But his reign of terror was short, ending when Puritan clergy (although not denying the existence of witches) attacked his methods and motives.

Tradition says that in 1647 Hopkins himself was convicted of witchcraft and hanged – but he is also said to have died peacefully in his bed or to have fled to New England.

Matthew Hopkins, the self-appointed 'Witchfinder General', profited only briefly from England's last serious outbreak of 'witch mania'.

Hopkins's victims are forced to name their 'familiars', devilish servants in the form of animals: cat, dog, hare, weasel – and horned greyhound.

A witch feeds her 'familiars', including two huge toads. Some alleged the demonic beasts fed from supernumary nipples on the witch's body.

A written curse is pinned to an image of the person to be harmed. This curse doll, or 'poppet', may date from the 18th century.

If she drowns, she is innocent: if she floats, guilty. A treatise of 1613 illustrates the cruel ordeal of 'swimming' for a suspected witch.

FACT FILE

❑ Like Red-hunting Senator McCarthy in the 1950s, Hopkins gained credibility by publicly displaying 'secret documents'; in his case, what he claimed to be the 'Devil's List', written in code by Satan himself, naming all England's witches.

❑ Those who hanged witches were themselves breaking England's witchcraft laws, the mildest in Europe. They forbade torture, and the Witchcraft Act of 1563 prescribed death only for those guilty of murder by sorcery. No English witches were burned: that penalty was reserved for heretics and traitors.

❑ During the English Civil War, Parliamentarians alleged that Prince Rupert of the Rhine (above), the Royalist cavalry leader also noted for his scientific experiments and inventions, was a witch, and that his poodle dog 'Boy' (who rode into battle on his saddle and was at last killed in action) was his familiar. Royalists replied that Oliver Cromwell had a pact with Satan – and had been seen taking tactical advice from a demon before his victory at the battle of Naseby in 1645.

Witch mania in Massachusetts

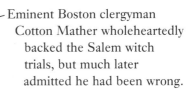

Eminent Boston clergyman Cotton Mather wholeheartedly backed the Salem witch trials, but much later admitted he had been wrong.

The 'bewitched' children of Salem: a scene from the 1957 movie *The Crucible*, based on Arthur Miller's play equating the trials with 1950s' McCarthyism.

In North America's first documented witch trial in 1648, Margaret Jones was condemned at Plymouth, Mass. Some 20 more New England witches were hanged before America's greatest outbreak of witch mania began in Salem Village (now the Boston suburb of Danvers) in 1689. It was a result of childish makebelieve. After hearing West Indian Voodoo tales from a black servant, Tituba, pastor's daughter Betty Parris (9), Abigail Williams (11) and other girls claimed that evil spirits were tormenting them. Rev. Samuel Parris and physician William Griggs decided they were bewitched, and the girls, having gone too far to back down unpunished, named the 'witches' responsible: Tituba, 'bag lady' Sarah Good and elderly invalid Sarah Osburn. Afraid for her life (she was spared, but sold into slavery to pay trial expenses), Tituba confessed that she and others in the community had made pacts with Satan. The girls gave more names: soon some 150 persons from Salem and nearby were gaoled. At their trials the girls had hysterics when touched by the accused; saw 'yellow birds' bring messages from Satan; and swore they were threatened by the witches' astral bodies. Many 'witches' confessed – for most who would not were sentenced to death. Two persons died in gaol; 19 were hanged. But now the Salem girls began to accuse prominent persons: Rev. Samuel Willard, President of Harvard; Lady Phips, wife of the Governor. Assisted by Boston divine Increase Mather (1639-1723) – whose more credulous son Cotton Mather (1663-1728) had helped fuel the witch mania – Governor Phips ensured that magistrates ceased to accept 'spectral evidence'. Of 52 persons accused in 1693, only 3 were condemned (and later pardoned). The witch hunt ended – and by 1736 accusation of witchcraft was a criminal offence in Massachusetts.

A British woodcut from the time of the Salem trials shows witches presenting their infants to the Devil, either for unholy baptism or human sacrifice.

Uproar in court: George Jacobs kneels, pleading for his life, as his own granddaughter accuses him of witchcraft. He was hanged on August 19, 1692.

❑ Sarah Good was hanged on July 19, 1689. On the gallows she was urged to confess by witch hunter Rev. Nicholas Noyes. She cried: 'I am no more a witch than you are a wizard, and if you take away my life, God will give you blood to drink.' In 1717 Noyes died after a haemorrhage, choking to death on his own blood.

❑ 80-year-old Giles Cory, whose wife was convicted and hanged, refused to plead at his trial. To loosen his tongue he was subjected to 'pressing' beneath heavy stones, an ordeal dating from medieval Europe, and died under the torture.

❑ Many at nearby Andover were accused of witchcraft by the Salem girls, among them the town's chief magistrate, who fled the Colony. They also accused two dogs, which were hanged. But the girls left Andover abruptly when a 'worthy Gentleman from Boston' whom they attempted to accuse swore out a warrant for slander and demanded damages of £1,000 (perhaps £180,000 today).

❑ Cotton Mather's *Memorable Providences Relating to Witchcrafts and Possessions* (1689) said an unsupported confession 'after due examination' (i.e., after denial of food and sleep, and threats of torture) was enough for conviction: 'What needs now more witness or further Enquiry?' he asked.

'White' witches and 'black' magic

British warlock Aleister Crowley may have designed this seal for his own use as grand master of a modern magical cult. 'Baphomet' was one of his many aliases.

Modern practitioners of witchcraft – which many call Wicca (Anglo-Saxon: 'witch') – disassociate their 'neo-Pagan religion' and its 'white' magic from the 'black' practices of Satanism. Wicca owes much to anthropologist Margaret Murray (1863-1963), whose *Witch Cult in Western Europe* (1921) and later books taught that medieval witchcraft stemmed from a pre-Christian, matriarchal, fertility religion. Although most scholars now deny the existence of this 'old religion', with a 'Mother Goddess' and 'Horned God' (not Satan, but a nature spirit like the 'Green Man'), Murray's beliefs are accepted, for different motives, by many New Age cultists and some feminists. A witchcraft revival surfaced in the 1950s under the leadership of British 'witch king' Gerald Gardner (1884-1964). He called it 'a religion of love, pleasure and excitement', and his instructional manual, *The Book of Shadows*, attracted many: on his death it was estimated there were 5,000 witches in Britain – and Wicca is now said to have up to 50,000 practitioners in the U.S.A. But Gardner's enemies said he accepted too many of the teachings of black magician Aleister Crowley, a major influence on modern Satanism. Crowley was obsessed by 'sex magic', and it is claimed that many Satanists use their 'religion' as a cover for sexually degrading activity. The practices of Anton Szandor LaVey (b.1930; now 'retired'), who founded the California-based Church of Satan in 1966 and attracted as many as 25,000 disciples, were fairly mild: he declared the sinister sacrifices of the Black Mass 'outmoded'. Real danger may come not from 'organized' Satanism but from the climate of belief it creates. In the U.S.A. and elsewhere an increasing number of crimes are committed by persons claiming to be 'possessed' by Satan or his demons – and by killers who claim that their victims are agents of the Devil.

'Skyclad' (naked) witches dance at midnight around a bonfire in County Kerry, Ireland, in 1981. They hope to invoke the power of a monster inhabiting nearby Lough Leane.

Portrait of Anton LaVey, founder of California's Church of Satan in the 1960s. He appeared as 'Satan' in the movie *Rosemary's Baby* (1968).

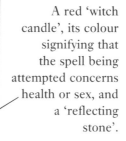

A red 'witch candle', its colour signifying that the spell being attempted concerns health or sex, and a 'reflecting stone'.

❏ Although there were no witch trials in Britain after c.1750, witchcraft remained a criminal offence there until 1951. Then, the Witchcraft Act of 1736 was replaced by the Fraudulent Mediums Act, aimed at those who worked scams by pretending to have magical powers.

❏ Perhaps the most successful modern witch was British-born Sybil Leek (1923-83), active in the U.S.A. from the 1960s. She made many T.V. appearances (usually with her pet jackdaw, 'Mr. Hotfoot Jackson'; her 'familiars' also included a boa constrictor) and wrote some 60 books on magic. At the time of her death she was said to be a millionaire.

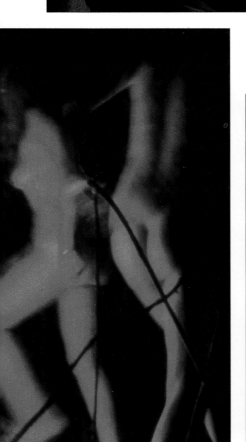

Magical ingredients on sale at a 'witch doctors' market', La Paz, Bolivia. 'New Age' interest in magic has seen stores like this flourish in North American and European cities.

❏ Anton LaVey's followers included movie star Jayne Mansfield (above). Her attorney Sam Brody quarrelled with LaVey, who cursed him – and in June 1967 warned Mansfield of danger if she continued to see Brody. A few days later the car in which Brody and Mansfield were driving hit a truck and both were killed.

Magic and the Third Reich

With 'Adolf Hitler is alive and well and living in California', a favourite tabloid sensation since 1945 has been 'Hitler was a black magician'. But Hitler's potent and deadly 'magic' lay solely in his own evil genius. He was prepared to pervert and exploit ancient occult lore, not to believe in it. The swastika emblem, originating in the Middle East before c.3000 B.C., was for millennia used worldwide (from ancient Egypt to the Navaho of North America) as a symbol of good fortune. In Nazi hands the *hakenkreuz* ('hooked cross') became, Hitler said, a symbol of 'the struggle for victory of the Aryan man'. The emergent Nazi Party took advantage of an upsurge in occult interest after World War I. It exploited alchemy, helping Munich alchemist Franz Tausend set up 'Company 164' to change base metals to gold. In 1931 the project collapsed. Tausend went to gaol: the Party banked a small fortune extracted from investors in the scam. Astrology was seen as a 'black propaganda' tool (fake horoscopes were used by both Axis and Allies) and Karl Ernst Krafft, often named as 'Hitler's astrologer', may never have met the *Führer*. Hitler's deputy Rudolf Hess may have been a believer: after his flight to Britain in 1941 astrologers thought to have influenced him were imprisoned; Krafft himself died in a concentration camp. One of Hitler's attempts to pervert an ancient mystery may have backfired. In 1938 he had the 'Holy Lance', supposedly the spear with which a Roman soldier pierced the side of the crucified Christ, removed from Vienna to Nuremberg. It was said to have been carried by the great Germanic leaders Charlemagne and Frederick Barbarossa – both, legend said, had died after mislaying it. On April 30, 1945, U.S. troops took possession of the Lance: hours later Hitler killed himself in Berlin.

The serviceman who wore this paid dearly for his swastika emblem: the Wound Badge in gold was awarded only for five or more wounds.

Although many had good reason to regard him as the Devil incarnate, Hitler had no personal belief in the occult.

Much of magic is ritual – and the Nazis were masters of ritual. Brownshirted stormtroopers' banners flank a rostrum with a giant swastika; Berlin, 1938.

As a mosaic decoration in an old Roman villa in Cyprus, the swastika means good luck. The Nazis made it a badge of shame.

Hitler's 'magical' oratory made evil seem good to many Germans. Here, he speaks at a pre-War May Day rally.

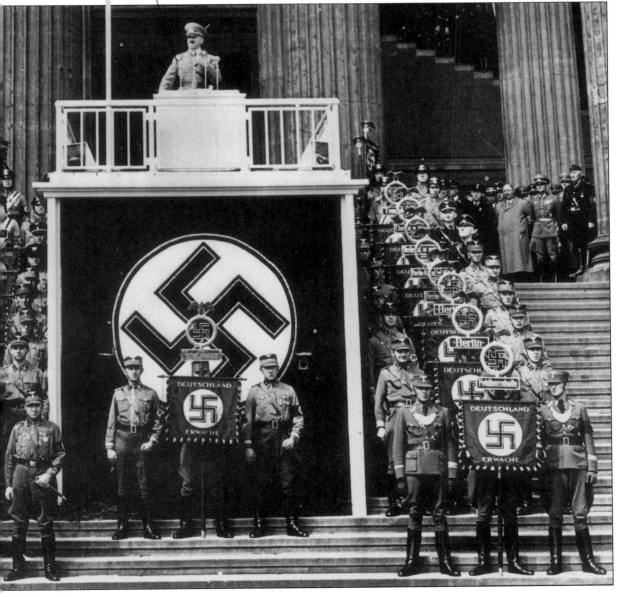

Fairy tales

Today we dismiss fairies as the stuff of children's stories. It was not always so. As recently as the 19th century fairies held much the same position in popular belief as space aliens do today: many folk were sceptical, but a fair number believed. Earlier, even learned men accepted fairies' existence – but not as the pretty, winged, 'little people' of traditional book illustrations. Fairies came in even more shapes and sizes than modern aliens: there were delicate elves, misshapen dwarfs, elusive leprechauns, savage trolls and many more. Most were feared as a powerful, even dangerous people midway between humans and devils – sometimes said to descend from fallen Angels not bad enough for Hell, but not good enough for Heaven. They lived underground, sometimes visiting the human world (usually invisibly) from hills or old grave mounds. Though they rewarded good treatment (those who put out a nightly bowl of milk for the sprites might find chores done in return), they were often mischievous or malignant. It was risky even to speak their name – people spoke instead of the 'good people', 'fair folk' or 'men of peace' – and many mysterious misfortunes were blamed on them. Rheumatism or cramps came from fairy blows and pinches; horses found off-colour in the morning had been ridden by fairies overnight. If a child ailed, its parents knew the fairies had stolen their healthy baby and left a substitute, or changeling – for they often took mortal children to raise as their own, or to sacrifice, in place of one of themselves, as the seven-yearly tribute they paid to Hell. Even adults were not safe. A sudden death might indicate a fairy kidnapping: the victim had been stolen away, and his or her apparent corpse was a 'stock', a dummy, left in its place.

The Dandelion Fairy.

In the 20th century, fairies, once seen as sinister beings, became pretty sprites in children's tales, as in this illustration of c.1920.

Found in the Pedro Mountains, Wyoming, in 1934, this 36cm (14in) tall mummy was once said to be proof of an ancient race of 'little people'. In fact, it is the body of a Native American infant.

'General Tom Thumb' (1838-83) and his wife Lavinia Warren (1841-1919) in 1863: some have theorized that persons of restricted stature were the original 'little folk'.

Fairies and gnomes look on as a craftsman elf goes to work: a fantasy illustration of the 1980s. Modern people like to escape into 'Fairyland', but their ancestors feared it.

FACT FILE

❑ When a Scottish labourer found a cache of 84 Norse chessmen on the Isle of Lewis in 1831, he dropped his spade and fled in terror, taking the still figures to be sleeping fairies. His tougher wife sent him back to get them – and the Lewis Chessmen (below) are now displayed in London's British Museum. But the Museum's guard dogs apparently agree with the finder: tradition says this is one exhibit they refuse to pass.

❑ The line between fairies and the souls of the dead was sometimes blurred. Cornish tin miners spoke of friendly goblins called Knockers, who led them to rich seams of ore. Perhaps these originated as nature spirits, but the miners said they were the souls of Jews, punished for their rejection of Christ with endless labour in the mines.

❑ World War II airmen with engine trouble turned, like their ancestors, to the supernatural for an explanation. Any mysterious problem was blamed on 'Gremlins' – modern goblins which aviators say specialize in technological sabotage.

'Sherlock Holmes' in Fairyland

Few Englishmen of his time were more popular than Sir Arthur Conan Doyle (1859-1930), creator of the great detective 'Sherlock Holmes'. A master of imaginative writing, he desperately wanted to believe in the paranormal – he was a leading supporter of Spiritualism and psychic research – but his bewitchment by the 'Cottingley fairies' brought him widespread ridicule. In July 1917, 16-year-old Elsie Wright of Cottingley, Yorkshire, took a photograph that appeared to show her 10-year-old friend Frances Griffiths with four tiny, winged 'fairies'. Frances photographed Elsie with a grotesque 'gnome'. Their parents assumed the girls had faked the pictures with cut-outs from books; the girls insisted the beck (stream) near their village was indeed alive with 'little people'. Mrs. Wright showed the photographs (five were taken in 1917-21) to psychical researchers – who pronounced them genuine. A medium sent by Doyle to investigate also saw fairies at the beck (but failed to photograph them) and decided the girls were 'natural mediums' who enabled 'elemental spirits' to materialize. Although even Elsie Wright's father said the great writer was 'bamboozled', Doyle proclaimed in the *Strand Magazine* that the fairies were proven fact, and published a full account in *The Coming of the Fairies* (1922). The kindest press comment on his credulity was that to attack such beliefs was like 'killing Santa Claus with statistics'. The sensation died, to be revived in the 1960s-70s when journalists rediscovered elderly Frances and Elsie. Elsie admitted that they had faked the photographs with cut-outs – but only after failing to take genuine photographs of the 'real' fairies. In a T.V. interview in 1976, Frances denied that the photographs were faked.

Many people noticed that the 'Cottingley fairies' closely resembled the dancing sprites in this contemporary advertisement.

William Marriott produced this fake to discredit 'the Cottingley hoax': a photograph of the 'Night Light' fairies is superimposed on one of Conan Doyle.

Price's Night Lights

Childs'
Royal Castle
Palmitine Star
Clarke's Pyramids

Frances Griffiths and the 'leaping fairy', one of the later photographs in the series. Elsie Wright claimed that she took this photograph from a distance of about 1m (3ft) in August 1920.

Popular fairy paintings like this – an illustration from a children's book of 1914 – may have originally inspired the Cottingley girls' prank.

Does it look convincing? Taken in July 1917, the first Cottingley photograph shows 10-year-old Frances with dancing fairies.

Doctor Johnson's strangest case

A hard-nosed realist but by no means a knee-jerk sceptic, Dr. Samuel Johnson, one of the most learned men of his time, proved an ideal 'ghost buster'.

In 1759 businessman William Kent and his mistress Frances ('Fanny') Lynes took rooms in the house of Richard Parsons in Cock Lane, City of London. Their stay ended in a quarrel when Parsons failed to repay a loan from Kent. The Kents moved to nearby Clerkenwell where, in February 1760, Frances died suddenly, officially from smallpox. Parsons claimed to have a vision of her as she lay dying, and very soon his 11-year-old daughter Elizabeth was plagued by a scratching, banging spirit. 'Talking' by a knocking code with Methodist minister John Moore it identified itself as 'Fanny' Lynes – poisoned by William Kent. Kent himself was made to come and hear, and angrily yelled: 'Thou art a lying spirit!' Fashionable London flocked to Cock Lane to hear 'Scratching Fanny', whose knocks, it is recorded, went on even when Elizabeth Parsons was put under restraint. A 'Committee of Gentlemen' was formed to consider whether Kent should be indicted for murder. It was headed by the age's most respected intellect, Dr. Samuel Johnson (1709-84). 'Fanny' promised to prove her bona fides by knocking on Frances Lynes's coffin in the crypt of St. John's Church, Clerkenwell. The Committee went there, Kent with them, and heard nothing. Johnson's opinion was that Elizabeth Parsons 'has some art of making or counterfeiting particular noises, and that there is no agency of any higher cause'. Then Elizabeth was caught in bed with a board on which she made knocks and scratchings. The child was spared punishment, but Parsons and his wife were imprisoned for conspiracy and Moore heavily fined. But many still believed in 'Scratching Fanny' – and when what was said to be Frances Lynes's coffin was opened in 1803 the body showed no trace of smallpox, but was in a condition of adipocere (a sign of arsenic poisoning).

The interior of the Rectory at Epworth, Lincolnshire – now a museum to the founder of Methodism – where John Wesley and his family experienced poltergeist activity in 1715-16.

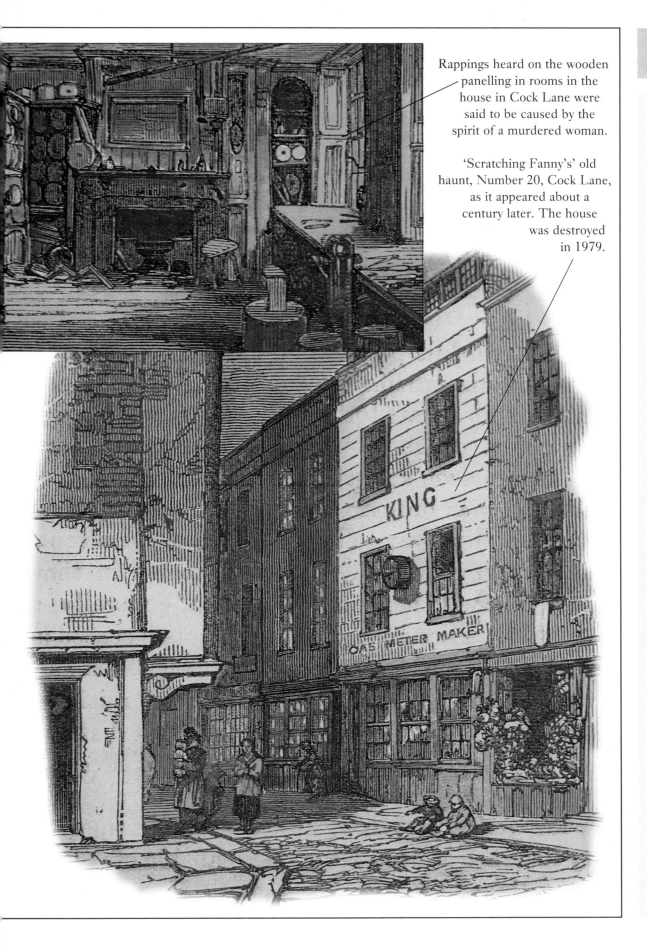

Rappings heard on the wooden panelling in rooms in the house in Cock Lane were said to be caused by the spirit of a murdered woman.

'Scratching Fanny's' old haunt, Number 20, Cock Lane, as it appeared about a century later. The house was destroyed in 1979.

❏ Moore's way of communicating with 'Scratching Fanny' was like that described by Johnson's friend John Wesley (1703-91), founder of Methodism. Wesley wrote an account of a spirit that plagued his father's rectory (below) at Epworth, Lincolnshire, in 1715-16, when the family heard loud knockings by 'Old Jeffrey'. Although noisy and liable to hurl objects around, the entity only once offered violence: when the Rev. Samuel Wesley challenged the 'deaf and dumb devil' to confront him, he was rudely shoved aside.

❏ Richard Parsons made good money from fashionable folk who came to hear the Cock Lane knockings. Within weeks of his trial, another 'knocking ghost' began performances near the Bow Street court of magistrate Sir John Fielding. When Fielding threatened that those responsible would 'knock hemp in Bridewell' (be put to hard labour in gaol) the ghost swiftly fell silent.

The real 'ghostbusters'

Hereward Carrington, among the S.P.R.'s leading researchers in c.1900-20, made a special study of 'projection of the astral body'.

When Lady Palmer photographed her friend Miss Townsend in a chapel at Domrémy, France, in 1925, two 'phantom priests' appeared in the background.

Scientific investigation of the supernatural began in 1882, when Frederick Myers, Edmund Gurney and other academics at Cambridge University founded the Society for Psychical Research (S.P.R.). An American S.P.R. was formed in 1884 under Harvard philosopher-psychologist William James (1842-1910). Early research focused on Spiritualist mediums, but soon widened to include ghosts and – with the work of Professor J.B. Rhine at Duke University, N.C., in the 1920s-30s – 'parapsychology': a word coined by Rhine to embrace E.S.P. and other 'wild talents'. Throughout their history the S.P.R. and A.S.P.R. have been attacked from all sides. Believers claim their preoccupation with scientific proof, which has always relied much on the camera and now uses state of the art electronics, is inimical to such a sensitive subject. Sceptics say they too readily accept evidence that may be faked (and in that category might include the 'ghost' photographs reproduced here). The U.S.A.'s top psychic research body today is the Parapsychological Association, founded 1957 and in 1969 affiliated to the American Association for the Advancement of Science. The major organization of 'ghostbusting' sceptics is the Buffalo-based Committee for the Scientific Investigation of Claims of the Paranormal (C.S.I.C.O.P.; or 'Psi-Cop'), which claims all 'supernatural' phenomena either have a scientific explanation or are fraudulent.

'It may well be the most genuine ghost photograph we possess,' said an S.P.R. spokesman. The 'Brown Lady' of Raynham Hall, Norfolk, England – an apparition reported many times – was captured as a misty, veiled figure by a photographer in 1936.

If, as many experienced psychic researchers believe, this picture is genuine, it ranks among the classics. The ghostly nun materialized at a séance in Lisbon in 1918.

A 'phantom hand' clasps the waist of Vernon D'Cruz of Adelaide, Australia, in this 1975 photograph. His family later said the picture was a hoax – but no one has yet explained how it was done.

Harry Price, ghost hunter

Harry Price (1881-1948), Britain's top ghost hunter, took a scientific approach: he pioneered the use of remote control movie cameras to record phenomena, and in 1926 established a National Laboratory of Psychical Research in London. But fellow S.P.R. members criticized his objectivity – and to sceptics he was often a figure of fun. His association with Austrian mystic Baron von Schrenk-Nötzing (nicknamed 'Shrink-from-nothing') was said to prove his credulity; so was his attempt, with eccentric philosopher C.E.M. Joad, to turn a white goat into a man by means of magic rites on Germany's 'haunted' Brocken Mountain in 1932. In 1936 he attracted more derision by appearing to endorse 'Gef, the talking mongoose', when a family on the Isle of Man claimed their daughter's imaginary pet had materialized and entertained them with conversation and song.

Price's major investigation was of 'England's most haunted house': Borley Rectory, Suffolk, built in 1863 on the site of a much older building. For decades its owners, clergymen and their families, reported hauntings: sounds of bells, voices, footsteps, knockings; sightings of a phantom coach and horses, a headless monk, a spectral nun; and many poltergeist incidents. Price recorded as many as 2,000 'happenings' in 1930-35 alone, when the house was occupied by the Rev. Lionel Foyster and his wife Marianne. In 1937-38 Price himself lived in the Rectory, and decided the disturbances were caused by the spirit of a 14th century nun who had been strangled at the site. In 1939 the Rectory was destroyed by fire: according to its new owner, caused by a poltergeist throwing books at an oil lamp. In 1943 Price claimed to have unearthed part of a woman's skull in the ruins, and it is said that when this was reverently buried in 1945 Borley's ghosts ceased to walk.

British psychic researcher Harry Price, seen here with one of his gadgets, pioneered the use of electronic aids for 'ghost hunting'.

Price left his collection of c.17,000 occult volumes to London University. The 'Harry Price Library' is now a Mecca for researchers.

'England's most haunted house', Borley Rectory, is seen just after it was wrecked by a fire, said to have been caused by a malevolent poltergeist, in March 1939.

Human remains found at Borley in 1943 – said by Harry Price to be those of a nun murdered there – are given Christian burial in 1945.

Harry Price (right) and philosopher Cyril Joad (1891-1953) prepare to work ritual magic on Germany's Brocken Mountain, 1932. The much derided experiment may have simply been a stunt to publicize Price's more serious work.

FACT FILE

❏ For his Brocken ritual (which he said was derived from an ancient magical text), Price needed a 'pure maiden'; a potion of soot, honey, rust from church bells and bat's blood; and a full Moon. The maiden was soon found – but it proved hard to catch bats, and the Moon obstinately remained veiled in mist. The rite failed, and Price and Joad claimed they had only tried it to show that ritual magic did not work.

❏ In 1979, 80-year-old Marianne Foyster, widow of Rev. Lionel Foyster, told members of the S.P.R. that although some truly supernatural things had happened, her husband had faked many of the poltergeist incidents recorded by Price at Borley Rectory. At the time Price himself had suspected that 'disturbed' Marianne Foyster might be faking phenomena, including 'spirit messages' to her that appeared on the Borley Rectory walls (below).

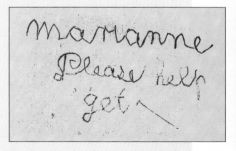

❏ London University ignored Price's plea to establish a psychical research fellowship, but he left it his collection of 17,000 books on the occult.

Poltergeists, the unquiet spirits

Poltergeist disturbances often involve teenagers. Uproar at a French farm in 1849 ceased after 14-year-old maidservant Adolphine Benoit was subjected to exorcism.

The most common of all 'ghosts', reported worldwide for many centuries, are those known as poltergeists (from the German words for 'noisy spirits'). It is an apt name, for poltergeists most often manifest themselves in noise-making activities: loud scratchings or knockings; sounds that may be interpreted as human speech; or the violent displacement of objects. They may be simply mischievous, breaking the odd plate or scribbling on walls; but sometimes seem malevolent, hurling heavy furniture, setting fires, or wrecking houses (as in the celebrated case of the Martin family of Methuen, Mass., driven from two houses in 1963 when poltergeists caused flash floods in their rooms, even when water mains were turned off and pipes drained). Do these activities sound rather like those of delinquent children? Some experts believe this is just what they are, theorizing that 'psychokinetic forces' generated by disturbed youngsters (particularly by the latent sexual energy of adolescents) are linked to such disturbances. The activities of the most famous American poltergeist, the 'Bell Witch' of Adams, Tenn., centred on teenage Betsy Bell in 1817-20. Hundreds claimed to have heard or witnessed the insults and pranks of a spirit that identified itself as 'Old Kate', most aimed at Betsy's father, John. Matters took a sinister turn when John died – and his family claimed that medicine prescribed for him had been switched for poison by the spirit. Later researchers have suggested that John (whom most contemporary accounts describe as a good man and loving father) perhaps may have treated Betsy cruelly, and that, consciously or unconsciously, she summoned up 'Old Kate' to punish him.

As well as hurling household goods around, poltergeists may use fire or water to achieve their destructive ends. This damage to a home in Brazil was caused by fire started by a poltergeist.

In 1985, when this home at Chester, England, was wrecked by poltergeist activity, its occupants received messages via computer from a man who had lived in the 16th century.

Poltergeists infesting a home in Mulhouse, France, 1978-81, produced these graffiti on a piece of paper inside a sealed camera from which film had vanished.

England's screaming skulls

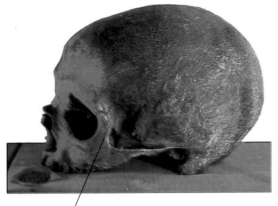

If the skull of Ambrose Barlow, a Roman Catholic priest martyred in 1641, is removed from Wardley Hall, England, screams and thunderclaps are heard.

Ancient peoples kept severed human heads in their homes as war trophies; sometimes as family relics, as we keep photographs of relatives; and often to ward off evil. Some English houses still hold guardian skulls which legend says have a life of their own. Bettiscombe Manor, Dorset, has one of the most famous, a skull said to shriek 'like a trapped rat' when moved, to rattle by night in ghostly bowling games – and to have heralded World War I by sweating blood. Several owners tried to scrap the grim relic: some reinstated it when local disaster ensued; others were thwarted by the skull itself, which returned whether thrown into a pond or buried deep in the ground. Legend variously says it is the skull of a murdered girl, or of an 18th century black slave whose master failed to return his body to Africa for burial; scientists say it is prehistoric. The screaming skull of Burton Agnes Hall, Yorkshire, truly belongs there. Anne Griffith, whose father built the Hall in c.1590, so loved her home that on her deathbed she asked her family to keep her head there – and haunted them with dreadful noises when they tried to disobey. The skull (nicknamed 'Owd Nance') screamed horribly if removed, and Anne's ghost walked the house to guard the relic – until, in 1900, the owners allayed her fears by building it into one of the walls. Theophilus Brome (d.1670) was equally set on keeping his skull at his house, Higher Chilton Farm, Somerset, where it remains today. But as a Puritan he may have been motivated less by love of his home than the wish to thwart Royalist supporters, who celebrated the Restoration of King Charles II by digging up dead Roundheads to exhibit their heads on stakes. Long after such risk was past, Brome's skull is said to have made 'horrid noises . . . of sad displeasure' when anyone tried to move it.

Now some fear the skull ('death's head') because it reminds us we all must die; in former times folk kept ancestral skulls as venerated relics.

Burton Agnes Hall, Yorkshire, England, still looks as stately as in this view of 1879. Since 1900 one of its walls has entombed the skull of 'Owd [Old] Nance'.

At his own wish, the clothed skeleton of philosopher Jeremy Bentham (d.1832) is now kept on display at University College, London – where his ghost is said to walk in times of trouble.

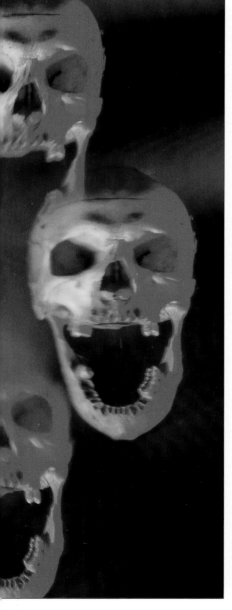

FACT FILE

❏ Once she had won her case to keep her head in Burton Agnes Hall, Anne Griffith proved a helpful ghost. Men who opened her coffin to remove the head found their unpleasant job had been done for them. The body was in perfect condition, but the head was already severed – and reduced to a clean skull.

❏ For some years the skeleton of local murderer William Corder was displayed in a Bury St. Edmunds' (Suffolk) hospital. When anyone approached, a spring-loaded mechanism triggered by pressure on a floor plank made the skeleton raise its arm and point to a box inviting charitable donations.

❏ European settlers who took the belief in 'guardian skulls' to America included the Pews, who came to Louisiana from France in the 1600s. Their house boasted a screaming skull nicknamed 'Ferdinand', supposed to be that of a medieval ancestor burned as a heretic – although a surgeon who examined it thought 'Ferdinand' was probably a Native American from Florida.

❏ In 1887 an Oxford professor visiting remote Merioneth, Wales, found a huge, dog-like skull by a lake. Intrigued, he took it back to his holiday cottage – to spend a night of terror while a wolfish monster with human eyes prowled outside. In the morning he threw the skull into the lake.

No earthly harbour: ghost ships old and new

In 1821 the *Edinburgh Magazine* published an anonymous ghost story: *Vanderdecken's Message Home*. It told of a Dutch sea captain who swore an ungodly oath to round the Cape of Good Hope if it took to all eternity. For his blasphemy he was condemned to sail on forever, bringing bad luck to all who sighted him. The tale inspired Wagner's opera *Der fliegende Holländer* (1843) – and launched the world's most famous ghost ship, the 'Flying Dutchman'.

For a spectre with its origin in fiction, the 'Dutchman' has attracted a surprising number of sightings. Few witnesses to any ghost outrank Britain's King George V (1865-1936), who, as a young naval officer in 1881, saw the ship in her most common haunt off the Cape. The officer who recorded the sighting in the log of HMS *Bacchante* – 'a strange red light . . . a ship all aglow . . . some 200 yards distant' – died mysteriously soon afterwards. Sightings of the 'Dutchman' and other ghost ships have been attributed to mirage, a trick of light refraction which can produce a 'ghostly' image of a real vessel many miles away. This cannot fully explain the apparition of a 4,300 tonne nuclear powered attack submarine. On April 10, 1963, USS *Thresher* failed to surface from deep diving trials east of Cape Cod; 129 men died in the worst submarine disaster of all time. In July 1967, cruising the same waters in the yacht *Yorktown Clipper*, Boston businessman John S. Schultz and his family saw a huge submarine surface nearby, briefly rise a few feet above the waves, fold up 'like a jackknife', then disappear. From the serial numbers clearly visible on her sail (conning tower), Schultz later identified the ghost ship as *Thresher*.

Artist Gustave Doré produced this engraving (1873) of one of fiction's most ghastly ghost ships: the ice-bound vessel described in Samuel Taylor Coleridge's *Rime of the Ancient Mariner* (1798).

Sailors show horror as the 'Flying Dutchman' is sighted. The picture dates from the 19th century, when the legend became popular, but tales of ghost ships are old as seamanship itself.

Modern technology provides no protection from the phantoms of the sea: a German World War I U-boat like this is said to have been haunted to its destruction.

The young naval officer later to become Britain's King George V claimed he saw the 'Flying Dutchman'. No one suggested he should tell that to the Marines!

93

The haunted White House

If the sites of great and violent events are those most likely to be haunted, it is no surprise that the White House, Washington, D.C., has its ghosts. Its very name is connected with an act of violence: its grey Virginia stone was painted white to cover scorch marks made by British troops who set it afire in the War of 1812. John Adams (2nd President; 1796-1800) moved in while the mansion was still building. His wife Abigail found the place comfortless and dirty – which is, perhaps, why her ghost has been seen hard at work on laundry in the East Room. Another unquiet First Lady is Dolley Madison (1768-1849). It is said that in 1917, when President Wilson's wife Edith ordered the rose garden Dolley had planned to be moved, Mrs. Madison put in an appearance that scared away the gardeners. But the presence most often felt is that of Abraham Lincoln, whose administrations saw much violence and ended tragically. The Lincolns' 12-year-old son Willie died in the White House, where his ghost was later reported by members of President Grant's family. Lincoln's ghost was often seen near his grave at Oak Ridge Cemetery, Springfield, Ill.; his first appearance (he had earlier been heard and sensed) at the White House was when Grace Coolidge, wife of President Calvin Coolidge (in office 1923-29), saw him standing at a window in the Oval Office. During World War II Lincoln appeared to Queen Wilhelmina of the Netherlands (a convinced Spiritualist) in her White House bedroom. When she told President Franklin Roosevelt, he calmly replied that Mrs. Roosevelt and many others had seen or heard the ghost in or near the room – and one of his secretaries had seen Lincoln sitting on the bed there, putting on his boots.

Designed by Daniel Chester French and dedicated in 1922, this massive, seated figure at the Lincoln Memorial, Washington, D.C., is an ever-present reminder of the 16th president, whose spirit walks the White House.

94

Tranquil under the floodlights: but many inhabitants of the White House – among them Presidents Ulysses S. Grant, Theodore Roosevelt and Herbert Hoover – reported 'ghostly' happenings there during their terms of office.

Abigail Adams, wife of 2nd President John Adams, was the first First Lady to live in the White House, 1800. She found the new mansion uncomfortable: her spirit, it is said, still tries to clean it up.

Abraham Lincoln's presence is the one most often experienced in the White House. He has been seen in the Lincoln Bedroom, shown here, and looking from a window in the Oval Office.

FACT FILE

❑ Mary Todd Lincoln became a devotee of Spiritualism and held séances in the White House. On one occasion a medium is said to have levitated a grand piano while Lincoln himself and two other men sat on it. After Lincoln's death a photographer called William Mumler photographed a widow in deep mourning. When the plate was developed it showed the ghostly figure of Lincoln standing behind her (below). The widow then admitted she was Mary Todd Lincoln – which Mumler (who was later ruined by accusations of trickery) claimed he had not known.

❑ Hard-headed President Truman once said in a T.V. interview that Lincoln's ghost had knocked on his bedroom door – but later insisted that he had been joking.

Victims of violence

Comparatively few well attested hauntings are recorded in connection with the Civil War, most violent episode in U.S. history. Of all its battlefields, the only one where ghostly soldiers have often been seen is Shiloh (Pittsburg Landing), Tenn., where more than 20,000 Union and Confederate soldiers died on April 6-7, 1862. But Shiloh's first 'ghosts' appeared soon after the War – and were all too real. Ex-Confederates who formed a *Kuklos* (Greek: circle; i.e. club) in Pulaski, Tenn., wore white robes and hoods to hide their identity. Superstitious folk murmured that the mystery men were ghosts of Confederate dead from Shiloh – and *Kuklos* extremists used the legend to launch the terror of the Ku Klux Klan. Other American victims of violence whose ghosts have been heard (but not seen) include 52 passengers from Mississippi riverboat *Iron Mountain*. New Orleans bound from Vicksburg, Miss., the 55m (180ft) craft vanished without trace in June 1872. Many believe she was broken up, and all aboard murdered, by river pirates: there are periodic reports from Vicksburg, Natchez and St. Joseph of agonized cries for help from the river, in the French Creole patois of *Iron Mountain*'s female passengers. Weapons made by the famous Winchester company played a major part in America's violent history. This so troubled Sarah L. Winchester (1838-1922) that she spent $20,000,000 in building and maintaining a huge mansion to 'shelter the spirits' of those killed by Winchester arms. The 'Winchester Mystery House' in California's Santa Clara Valley is a maze of 160 rooms (many with 13 windows), connected by 40 stairways (most with 13 steps). Sarah lived there for 36 years (except for a 6-year break when, believing a new Flood was due, she moved to a luxury houseboat), regularly giving banquets for 13: herself and 12 ghostly guests.

Reflecting the state's long, often violent history, many of the colonial mansions of Virginia – like 'Edgewood', Charles City, seen here – are reputed to be haunted.

The sprawling 'Winchester Mystery House' at San Jose, Cal., was built over a period of some 38 years by Sarah Winchester as a haven for the spirits of those killed by Winchester armaments.

In the 19th century psychic Edward Wyllie went looking for America's ghosts with his camera. Results included this photograph of c.1890.

Early victims of their vicious activities were cowed by rumours that Ku Klux Klan thugs were the ghosts of Confederate soldiers.

❏ Many have reported seeing the ghostly appearance of the two trains (below) – one of seven cars draped in black, complete with spectral musicians playing funereal airs; the other a single flat car with a coffin – that in 1865 carried the body of assassinated President Lincoln from Washington, D.C., to his burial place at Springfield, Ill. In 1876 grave robbers almost succeeded in snatching Lincoln's remains; later, a new tomb was built in which the President and his First Lady lie 4m (13ft) deep, their coffins embedded in concrete.

❏ Sunshine Skyway Bridge, Tampa Bay, Fla., is said to be one of America's accursed structures. Some 50 people have leapt to their deaths from it since its opening in 1954; around 55 lives were lost in a series of four shipping disasters at the bridge in January-May 1980. Locals claim the 6.5km (4mi) long structure is hexed by the spirit of a construction worker accidentally entombed in its foundations during building.

Stranger than truth

Tabloid hype made a home on Long Island infamous in the 1970s. But the house seen here in a still from *The Amityville Horror* (1979) was a 'stand in'.

In two of the U.S.A.'s best known supernatural cases of recent years, fiction – aided by media hype – has proved stranger than truth. The movie *The Exorcist* (1973) was 'based on reality'; in fact, on a minor poltergeist case. In 1949 the Washington, D.C., home of Douglas Deen (14) was plagued by the kind of poltergeist activity associated with highstrung teenagers. After exorcism by a priest, the disturbances ceased. Author William Peter Blatty wove a fine horror tale around the incident – but did not pretend that his 'possessed' girl, levitating and contorting, and her resident demon that mocked the horrified exorcist, were anything but fiction. But many people believe the 'true story' – and probably even more credit 'Amityville'. No one denies that on November 13, 1974, at 112 Ocean Avenue, Amityville, L.I., Ronald DeFeo, Jr. (24) shot to death six members of his family. He pleaded insanity, but was given six life sentences. What is questioned is what followed the purchase of the 'death house' by George and Kathy Lutz. They fled after 26 days' residence in December 1975-January 1976, alleging malignant poltergeist activity and attempted 'possession'. George, they said, had begun to resemble Ronald DeFeo; Kathy had levitated and had been temporarily transformed into an old, hideous crone. The late Jay Anson's account of their ordeal, *The Amityville Horror*, made a bestselling book and blockbusting movie. After thorough investigation the respected American Parapsychological Association declared the tale 'mostly fiction', but it still prospers and grows. Lately, amateur ghost hunters have 'proved' the Amityville house stands over an ancient Native American burial ground; and that an inhabitant of a house on the site in the 1700s practised black magic in the basement, on the spot where Ronald DeFeo established a red-painted 'den'.

Priests watch in helpless amazement as the body of a young girl possessed by the Devil rises aloft: a scene from *The Exorcist* (1973). Writer William Peter Blatty based his story on a real incident.

If 'emotionally resonant' places are the most likely to be haunted, then Alcatraz Island, San Francisco Bay, site of America's most famous top security prison in 1934-62, should be infested by spooks.

Fear of possession by demons has long haunted humanity. *The Bible* tells us how Jesus himself performed the rite of exorcism, seen here in a 10th century ivory carving.

SUPERFACTS

Fending off fiends

Since ancient times people have invented various protections against the Devil. Citizens of ancient Babylon kept off demons with a 'devil trap' buried under their homes: an inverted bowl, inscribed with a magical text. A typical example of c.300 B.C. proclaims a 'bill of divorce' to the Devil and all his night monsters, and orders them to leave the community. An alternative approach adopts low cunning rather than demon-repellents. Even today, some Maltese churches have two clocks, one set to the right time, the other not – to confuse the Devil about the times of church services.

Beating the demon

According to the Apocryphal *Book of Tobit*, Asmodeus – demon of lust, whose task is to stir up trouble between married couples – strangled the first seven husbands of Tobias's wife, Sarah, to prevent the consummation of the marriage. Tobias and Sarah fooled the demon by refraining from intercourse for the first three nights of their marriage. In peasant communities in Europe, this custom of 'Tobias Nights' was observed until as late as the 19th century.

Heavenly mountains ▶

Many peoples located the home of their gods atop sacred mountains – like Mount Olympus, where the Greek gods were held to live, and Mount Fuji (right) in Japan. In India, Mount Meru was the home of sky god Indra; and Mount Kailasa the paradise of Hindu god Shiva. The Chinese long believed they could reach the gods by climbing sacred mountains, and Chinese pilgrims still toil up holy Mount Taishan. In ancient Sumer worshippers built artificial 'mountains' as homes for their gods, in the form of mighty towers called ziggurats.

Not so Good Book

Emperor Menelik II (1844-1913) of Ethiopia did much to modernize his then backward nation, but the progressive ruler had his own superstitions. He believed that he could preserve his health by periodically eating chapters from *The Bible* – and is said to have

died when he attempted to counter the effects of a heart attack with an overdose of the *Book of Kings*.

◀ Telling the old, old story

The fullest version of the *Epic of Gilgamesh* (left), the Assyrian, was written on 12 clay tablets, with c.300 lines to each. Fragments of all 12 survive, most from Nineveh's library:

Infernal inspiration

The Italian composer Giuseppe Tartini (1692-1770) incurred the wrath of the Church when he wed a Cardinal's niece without permission. He hid out, of all places, in a monastery – where one night the Devil appeared to him, picked up his violin, and played a piece of music. When he recovered from the shock of his

Cooler in Hell

Irreverent scientists have pointed out that, on Biblical evidence, Heaven must be hotter than Hell. *Revelations* (Ch.1; v.28) describes Hell (left) as 'the lake which burneth with fire and brimstone' – and the boiling point of brimstone (above which it becomes a gas, not a liquid) is 445°C. (832°F.). In Heaven, according to *Isaiah* (Ch.30; v.26), 'the light of the sun shall be sevenfold', which it is estimated will give a celestial temperature of about 495°C. (950°F.).

Divine architect

The first pyramid – and Egypt's first great stone building – was the Step Pyramid at Saqqara, built c.2700 B.C. as the tomb of King Zoser. One thousand years later its architect, Imhotep, was declared a god – one of the few persons other than pharaohs thus honoured in Egypt. Imhotep was learned in medical science as well as architecture, and centuries later the Greeks identified him with Asclepius, god of medicine.

Tracks of tears

Not only images of Christ, the Virgin and saints have been known to 'weep', often bloody tears (below). On August 6, 1945, the day of the atomic bombing of Hiroshima, the bronze figure of a Japanese girl owned by Allen Demetrius of Pittsburgh, Pa., shed tears which left green streaks still visible many years later. More recently, sceptical U.S. scientist Shawn Carlson has devised six ways to make images 'weep' convincingly.

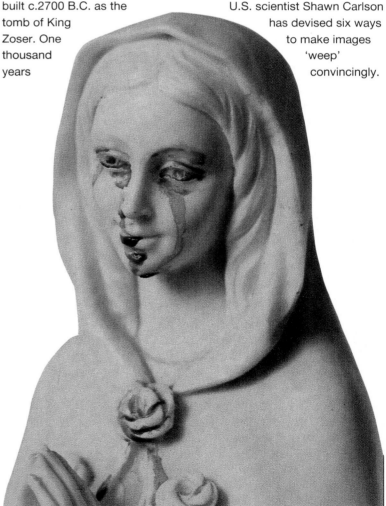

vision, Tartini wrote down the infernal composition as a sonata, the *Trillo del Diavolo* ('Devil's Trill'). It is still a popular item in the repertoire of violin virtuosi.

Onion eyes

To make corpses look their best, ancient Egyptian embalmers replaced missing teeth with false ones of ivory, filled out sparse hair with toupees, and repaired mutilations. A man who had lost his nose was given a wooden one, tied on with leather thongs; the bedsores of an old woman were patched with gazelle skin. Eye sockets were filled with artificial eyes of stone, linen, or, in the case of Ramesses IV, two small, painted onions.

SUPERFACTS

Practical Buddha

Enthusiasts for Eastern mysticism should perhaps consider the ancient legend of Buddha's visit to a yogi who lived by a river. The holy man proudly told Buddha that 25 years of fasting and meditation had given him the power to cross the water by levitating. But Buddha was not impressed. 'Surely,' he said, 'it would have been quicker to build a bridge!'

▼ Marketing Mithra

In the late 4th century A.D. Christianity triumphed over Mithraism – and left suppliers of Mithraic religious images with much unwanted stock on their hands. They soon relabelled their wares: unsaleable paintings of Mithra shooting arrows at a rock became Moses striking water from the rock; a minor adjustment transformed Mithra slaying the bull into Samson killing the lion.

The Green Man ▶

Celtic nature worship often used the motif known as the Green Man, or Jack-in-the-Green: a man's face with foliage growing from ears and mouth, thought to be some Celtic tree god. In the Middle Ages the Green Man became a popular subject in art, even in churches (right), and featured as a fertility symbol in mummers' plays, where his part was taken by a young man covered in branches – who was sometimes ducked in the river to ensure rain for the crops. In Britain today many inns bear the name of the Green Man, attesting to local fertility rites long forgotten.

War god in court

War god Mars was a favourite deity of the Romans, who claimed him as father of Rome's founder Romulus and believed he would always come to the aid of Romulus's descendants. His Greek equivalent, Ares, had no such close relationship with mortals, but was dreaded as

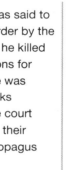

violent and cruel. He was said to have been tried for murder by the assembly of gods after he killed one of the sea god's sons for raping his daughter. He was acquitted; but the Greeks remembered this divine court case when they named their homicide court the Areopagus ('Hill of Ares').

Menace of the 'Rosy Cross' ▶

In 17th-18th century Europe the Rosicrucian movement provoked a reaction like the U.S.A.'s 'Red Scares' of the 1930s-60s. It was supposedly a mystic brotherhood of ancient times, re-founded by Christian Rosencreutz (1378-1484), and was rumoured to aim at world revolution led by an 'Invisible College' of master magicians. (Similar stories were told of the Order of Illuminati, founded by a Bavarian lawyer, Adam Weisshaupt, in 1776.) In fact, Rosicrucianism was a harmless cult, partly inspired by the 'Enochian magic' (right) of John Dee. Its major text,

The Chemical Wedding of Christian Rosencreutz (1616), was written by a clergyman as a literary joke. 'Rosy Cross' groups still exist, ranging from

serious students of alchemy to sects offering bogus 'correspondence courses' in occultism.

Prophetic trees ▶

At the centre of Norse mythology stood the World Tree, the ash Yggdrasil, which supported the entire universe. On this tree the god Odin (right) hung as a sacrifice to himself in his quest for wisdom. Long after the Norse gods were forgotten, the ash was honoured in Europe, and credited with curative and divinatory powers. The English believed if ash trees failed to produce their 'keys' (seeds) in autumn, this heralded the king's death or other national disaster. It was said no ash tree in England bore seed in 1649, the year King Charles I was beheaded.

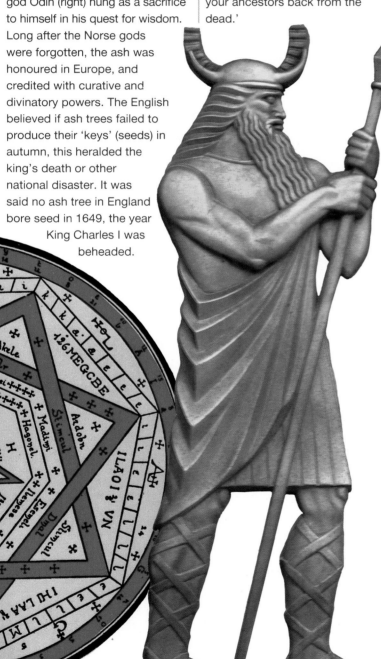

Miracle drink!

One aspect of an improvement in Sino-American relations in the 1980s was that a famous brand of cola went on sale in China. It is said that an advertising campaign had to be rethought when it was pointed out that the slogan '- - - - adds life' could be read in Chinese to mean: '- - - - brings your ancestors back from the dead.'

▲ Gaolbird's tale

The bestknown version of King Arthur's story is that of Sir Thomas Malory, completed in 1469. Malory described himself as 'a knyght presoner', so scholars believed he had been a noble prisoner of war – until research revealed he had served prison terms for assault, theft, extortion, cattle rustling and rape. Malory broke gaol twice – once swimming a moat; once fighting his way out 'armed with swords, daggers and halberds' – but after his last recorded arrest in 1460 seems to have stayed behind bars until his death in 1471. The 'noble and joyous book entytled *Le Morte Darthur*' ('The Death of Arthur') (above) was probably written in London's infamous Newgate Prison.

Double header

Supposed relics of King Arthur were a great draw in the 15th century: swords, cloaks, or Westminster Abbey's 'print of his seal in red wax'. Winchester Cathedral still displays a 'Round Table' – made in the 14th century and later repainted with Henry VIII's Tudor roses. Dover Castle once boasted the skull of Arthur's Sir Gawain. A critic pointed out that another castle also had Gawain's skull – a bigger one. Dover's custodians explained that was the skull of adult Gawain; their specimen was Gawain's skull when he was a boy.

SUPERFACTS

Wimpish witches ▶

Witches are apparently less tough today than in the Middle Ages. Medieval witches were said to rub on 'flying ointment', so they could be magically transported to Sabbats (right). Modern witches also grease their bodies – but only for weatherproofing when performing 'skyclad' (naked) rituals outdoors. Practices in California's Church of Satan include ritual flogging – but it is reported that worshippers are issued with protective clothing: padded shorts or panties.

▼ Grammar and glamour

Medieval writers called fairyland 'Land of Gramarye' – a mystic word which is actually our prosaic 'grammar'. Its first meaning, 'the art of writing', was corrupted in an age when writing seemed to many a magical skill, and came to signify occult knowledge. The

same word gave us *grimoire*, the sorcerer's secret handbook (left) – and 'glamour', originally a rather sinister enchantment. Fairies could 'cast a glamour' over the eyes of humans – making them mistake a handful of dead leaves for gold, or a hideous bugaboo for a lovely maiden. Cynics might say modern beauty products that promise 'magical' transformation provide the same kind of glamour.

Hairy fairies?

A 16th century British writer made a list of nearly 200 kinds of fairy and spirit. Among the odder names are shellycoats, mum-pokers, spoorns, flay-boggarts, gallytrots, gringes, bonelesses, Jinny-burnt-tails, clabbernappers and – admirers of the works of J.R.R. Tolkien may be surprised to learn – hobbits (but no orcs).

▼ Ancestral guilt

It is said that one of America's greatest writers owed both his name and inspiration for one of his works to the Salem witch trials. Nathaniel Hawthorne (1804-64) (below) was a descendant of John Hathorne, one of the judges who condemned the supposed Salem witches: the 'w' may have been added to the family's name in disapproval of their ancestor. Hawthorne's novel *The House of the Seven Gables* (1851) draws on the legend of Nicholas Noyes, a Puritan witch hunter cursed by one of his victims at Salem.

Actor's 'comeback' prevented ▷

Hungarian-American movie actor Peter Lorre (1904-64) (right) was noted for his sinister roles and appeared in several horror films. Soon after his death, police in Oklahoma arrested the leader of a group of Satanists who were alleged to be planning to dig up the actor's corpse and by evil ritual reanimate it.

Hidden hand

British witches of the 16th-17th centuries were believed to be able to move around unseen by using a 'Hand of Glory': a hand from the corpse of a hanged man, pickled and given Satanic baptism. It was said that if a candle was placed in the hand (or wicks attached to its tallowed fingers), anyone in its vicinity would fall into deep sleep so long as the light burned. Criminals saw this as a useful tool: as late as 1831 a gang of housebreakers in Ireland was caught in possession of a 'Hand of Glory'.

Another haunted 'White House'

The Octagon, Washington, D.C., built in 1800 and now the headquarters of the American Institute of Architects, served as temporary 'White House' for President Madison when British troops damaged the presidential mansion in 1814. It is said to be haunted by its builder Colonel John Tayloe, and by his daughter, who jumped to her death from the second floor landing when Tayloe forbade her marriage. Carpeting on the spot where she died is

regularly found rolled aside. The heavy footsteps of sorrowing Colonel Tayloe are often heard. The Octagon is also reputedly haunted by a servant girl who flung herself to death from its balcony to escape the unwelcome advances of a British officer during the War of 1812.

Travelling fairies ▷

Fairies are of European stock, carried abroad by early emigrants like the bemused Irishman (right). In Australia in the 1890s, revenue men arrested a Scottish immigrant family for making bootleg whisky. The moonshiners were not too surprised by their misfortune: the night before they had forgotten to set out the first 'draw' of spirit for the fairies, who naturally were annoyed and

withdrew their protection. Settlers also took fairy lore to America, where the only 'native' U.S. sprites, the 'little people' of some Native American tales, may derive from misunderstanding of the religious teachings of Jesuit missionaries.

Echoes of World War II

In April 1984 the pilots of two airliners over the Pacific some 290km (180mi) northeast of Japan's Honshu Island witnessed a 'nuclear explosion' reminiscent of the atomic destruction of Hiroshima in 1945. They saw a 'mushroom cloud' that within two minutes rose to about 18,290m (60,000ft), reached some 322 km (200mi) in diameter, then vanished. Investigation revealed no sign of radioactivity: scientists could only suggest 'meteoric activity'. Another 'echo' of World War II was the sighting of ghostly soldiers at Tokyo's Nari Shrine in 1979.

INDEX

Page numbers in **bold** indicate major references including accompanying photographs. Page numbers in *italics* indicate captions to illustrations. Other entries are in normal type.

Shells, beads and feathers make up a mask used in traditional ritual magic in Zaïre, Africa

PICTURE CREDITS

The publishers wish to thank the following agencies and individuals who have supplied photographs for this book. The photographs have been credited by page number and, where necessary, by position on the page: B(Bottom), T(Top), L(Left), BR(Bottom Right), etc.

The Ancient Art & Architecture Collection: 10, 16, 29(L)(R), 30, 35(TL), 37(TL), 40-1(T)(B), 44(TR)(BL), 45(BL)(L)(R), 48, 61(BL), 100

Art Resource: 10-11, 11(BL), 16-17, 20-1, 22-3, 24, 24-5, 26(R), 28, 31(TL), 35(R), 36-7(T)(B), 39(BR), 101(TL)

Art Resource/Erich Lessing: 17(L), 21(R), 32

Ashmolean Museum, Oxford: 66(L) (from Images Colour Library)

The Bettmann Archive: 25(R), 56, 62-3, 72(TR), 72-3, 79(T), 85(R), 89(R), 95(TL), 97(R), 104-5, 105(T)

Lee Boltin: 2-3, 13(BR), 30-1, 31(L), 50, 51(BL)(R), 52, 53(TL)(BL), 56-7, 58-9(T), 59(TL), 79(R)

Janet & Colin Bord: 17(BL), 47(R)

Dr. G.T. Meaden/Janet & Colin Bord: 39(T)

Bridgeman/Art Resource: 19(T), 47(TL), 67(BL)

British Museum: 61(TL)

Everett Collection, Inc.: 13(TL), 39(BL), 55(R), 73, 98, 99(T)

Fortean Picture Library: 14-15, 27(TL)(R), 46, 53(R), 71(B), 74-5, 85(BL), 101(BR)

Klaus Aarsleff/Fortean Picture Library: 75(B)

John Bonar/Fortean Picture Library: 78(L)

Philip Carr-Gomm/Fortean Picture Library: 43(R)

Dr. Elmar R. Gruber/Fortean Picture Library: 14, 26(L), 62, 64, 89(TR)

George Kanigowski/Fortean Picture Library: 15(TL)

Guy Lyon Playfair/Fortean Picture Library: 89(TL)

Lars Thomas/Fortean Picture Library: 96-7

Andreas Trottmann/Fortean Picture Library: 91(B)

Ken Webster/Fortean Picture Library: 88-9

F.P.G. International: 32-3, 48-9, 49(B), 54, 94-5, 95(BL), 98-9, 100-1

F.P.G. International/Jean Kugler: 65(T)

F.P.G. International/Buddy Mays: 52-3

Giraudon/Art Resource: 20, 21(L), 38-9, 68-9

Horizon/Douglass Baglin: 58

Horizon/Chun Shih: 65(B)

Images Colour Library: 5, 7, 11(TL)(R), 12(TR), 12-13, 15(BL)(R), 18; 18-19, 19(B), 21(BL), 22, 23(T)(B), 25(TL)(BL), 28-9, 31(R), 33(TL)(BL)(R), 34, 34-5, 36, 37(R), 38, 42, 42-3, 43(BL), 46-7, 47(BL), 50-1, 51(TL), 55(T), 57(B), 58-9(B), 60, 65(L), 66, 66-7, 67(TL)(R), 68, 69(T)(B), 70, 70-1, 71(T), 72(BL), 74, 75(T), 76(T), 77, 78(R), 79(B), 81(TL)(TR), 82(L), 83(TL)(BL)(R), 84(L), 84-5, 85(L), 90, 90-1, 92, 94, 95(R), 97(BL),

99(B), 102(BL)(TR), 102-3, 103(L), 104(T)(BL), 107

Philip Daly/Images Colour Library: 41

J.B. Pictures/Maggie Steber: 8, 63(BL)

Mary Evans Picture Library: 17(R), 26-7, 27(BL), 35(BL), 40, 43(TL), 55(BL), 57(T), 59(BR), 71(R), 81(BL)(BR), 82(R), 88, 91(T), 92-3, 93(BL)(R), 105(B)

Mary Evans/Alfred Pearse: 21 (TL)

Mary Evans/Harry Price Coll., Univ. of London: 60-1, 80(T)(B), 84(R), 86, 86-7, 87(BL)(TR)(R)

Mary Evans/Society for Psychical Research: 110-1

North Wind Picture Archives: 29(BL), 103(R)

Photo Researchers, Inc.: 63(TL)

Photo Researchers, Inc./R. Rowan: 12(BL)

Photo Researchers, Inc./Ulrike Welsch: 55(L)

Photri, Inc./Everette Evans: 96

Reuters/Bettmann: 63(R)

Royal Navy Submarine Museum: 93(TL)

Springer/Bettmann Film Archive: 75(R)

U.P.I./Bettmann: 49(TR), 61(R), 65(R), 76(B), 76-7, 97(L)

As his funeral took place, a camera 'saw' Lord Combermere in his library.